CAPITALIST SOLUTIONS

CAPITALIST SOLUTIONS

A Philosophy of American Moral Dilemmas

Andrew Bernstein

Transaction Publishers
New Brunswick (U.S.A.) and London (U.K.)

Library of Congress Catalog Number: 2011012370
ISBN: 978-1-4128-4294-5
Printed in the United States of America

Library of Congress Cataloging-in-Publication Data
Bernstein, Andrew.
Capitalist solutions : a philosophy of American moral dilemmas / Andrew Bernstein.
    p. cm.
Includes bibliographical references and index.
    ISBN 978-1-4128-4294-5
1. Capitalism—United States. 2. Capitalism—Moral and ethical aspects—United States. 3. United States—Economic policy—2009- 4. United States—Social policy—1993- 5. Environmental policy—United States. I. Title.
    HB501.B457 2012
    330.12'20973—dc22
            2011012370

To Lisa Doby,
Who Taught the Author
Life's Most Valuable Lesson

And to Penelope Joy Milano,
Who Fills Her Daddy's Life With Love

Contents

Acknowledgments

Many persons contributed to the completion of this book. Judith Rothman both recommended the manuscript to the publisher and provided the author with constant encouragement. The directors of Transaction, Irving Louis Horowitz and Mary Curtis, were similarly encouraging, and, indeed, coined the book's title.

The chapter on the necessity to privatize the American educational system originally appeared as an essay in the Winter 2011 issue of *The Objective Standard*. It is reprinted here with gratitude to Craig Biddle, founder and editor of *The Objective Standard*.

My good friend, Paul Saunders, provided invaluable editorial feedback, especially regarding the chapter on environmentalism and the claims of man-made global warming.

Finally, special thanks to the three great ladies of my life—Aline Bernstein, Regina Milano, and Lisa Doby—who put up with so much, for so long, as I puttered along my slow path to wisdom; and to one who will perennially be my leading lady, my beautiful daughter, Penelope Joy.

Introduction

Resolving the Country's Problems

To be blunt, the United States faces enormous challenges as it enters the second decade of the twenty-first century. Environmentalism and its claim of pernicious man-made global warming constitute one major issue; the danger from terrorism generated by Islamic Totalitarianism, a second; affordable, quality health care, a third. Additionally, education in America has remained an unresolved dilemma for decades. Nor do these issues exhaust the list. There are numerous others.

Currently, the United States Government pushes the nation remorselessly toward socialism in its attempt to resolve America's problems. Obamacare is one, but by no means only example of this. The government's increasing control of the banking industry, its massive bailouts of foundering auto makers, and its proposal of cap-and-trade are also examples of the same principle: an expansion of government's power—real or recommended—over the lives of individual American citizens.

But, in fact, whatever the delusions of the United States Government, morally upright and practically efficacious solutions come solely from moving to the opposite end of the political–economic spectrum: to full protection of individual rights and to establishment of laissez-faire capitalism. Individual rights and free markets are, in every case, the solution to America's problems.

In *Atlas Shrugged*, and in her nonfiction works, Ayn Rand developed a systematic body of thought, a comprehensive philosophy she dubbed "Objectivism." It is a revolutionary body of thought that has been sadly neglected by professional intellectuals for fifty years, but which, today, is finally, properly beginning to be seriously studied in academic philosophy departments. Objectivism provides the moral and philosophic validation of the political—economic principles of individual rights and free markets. Analysis of today's gravest issues

1

within the philosophic framework provided by Objectivism constitutes the single greatest hope of identifying rational solutions to these issues.

That is the goal this book seeks to accomplish. Consequently, it consists of two parts: (1) A brief introduction to the relevant principles of Objectivism. (2) A much longer section—the main part of the book—showing that and how Objectivism's validation of individual rights and free markets, applied to today's thorniest dilemmas, resolve those dilemmas both morally and practically.

Part One:
The Relevant Principles
of Objectivism

The Relevant Principles of Objectivism

A key original principle of Objectivism that will repeatedly emerge in this book is the identity of the moral and the practical. What is morally right is practically efficacious—and, conversely, what is morally wrong is practically disastrous.

The idea that only moral virtue leads to long-term practical success—and that evil, will, in the long run, accrue misery—opposes the dominant code of the modern world; which claims generally that callous exploitation of others is a necessary condition of practical success, while "selfless" virtue is too noble for this world, resulting in inevitable failure. The belief that "either you swim with the sharks or you're eaten by them" is widely held in such fields as law, business, politics, and others. Leo Durocher's cynical observation that "nice guys finish last" is, unfortunately, an accurate description of many people's belief on this topic.

An equation of virtue and practical success—and of vice with abysmal failure? How is such an innovative theory supported? The answer to this question penetrates to the heart of moral philosophy.

The proper name of Rand's moral code is: "rational egoism." Expressed briefly, this means that virtue is achieved by pursuing one's self-interest—that which leads to personal happiness—in accordance with rational moral principles. The key to Rand's version of rational egoism lies in understanding the nature of values, and the role they play in human life.

She defines values as: "that which one acts to gain and/or keep." A value is always the object of an action—it is not a wish, a dream, or a fantasy. An individual's values are those things or persons he considers preeminently worthy (or valuable); those things or persons that fill his life with meaning, passion, and purpose. Whether an individual values education, or a productive career in a specific field, or a particular man or woman, or his children, or a plethora of other possibilities, his values are those things or persons sufficiently important to him to impel him to goal-directed action.

The role of values in man's life is an overarching theme in Rand's fiction. In *The Fountainhead*, for example, its hero, the revolutionary architect, Howard Roark, is portrayed as so in love with his buildings that he literally cannot keep his hands off of them as they are under construction. The young Roark seeks mentoring from Henry Cameron, the world's greatest living architect, but a bitter, aging curmudgeon. Cameron, recognizing the young man's genius and integrity, becomes a father figure to the hero-worshipping Roark. The innovative young architect has a passionate love relationship with the tormented but brilliant and idealistic Dominique Francon, his eventual wife. He is more than friends—he is soul mates with the story's tragic hero, Gail Wynand. Roark rescues the talented young sculptor, Steven Mallory, from bitter despair and incipient alcoholism, and the budding genius goes on to become both a major success, and, in effect, Roark's kid brother.

The same is true in *Atlas Shrugged*, in which the two main narrators, Dagny Taggart, who superbly runs a transcontinental railroad—and Hank Rearden, the country's ablest steel manufacturer and inventor of Rearden Metal, a new alloy vastly superior to steel—are each passionately in love with their careers, and with each other.

In both Rand's great novels, and in her nonfiction work on ethical theory, *The Virtue of Selfishness*, she presents an integrated, impassioned theme: *Values are the meaning of life.*

To hold values dearly, to pursue them vigorously, and to never surrender them for any thing or any body—this is what it means to be genuinely, properly *selfish.* This is what is truly egoistic, i.e., in the interest of the ego or self; this is the sole course to personal happiness.

But a proper egoism does not consist of a relentless pursuit of any urge or desire an individual experiences. *Values, properly understood, are objective; not subjective whims.*

What makes X a value? What makes something good? This is a question that moral philosophers have debated for at least two millennia. Rand posed the question in a new form. She asked, in effect: what is the fundamental fact of reality that gives rise to the entire phenomenon of valuing? Her answer was: it is only because living beings must attain certain ends to sustain their lives that values become both necessary and possible. In the absence of life, there are no values; no possibility of either good or evil.

A plant, for example, must gain sunlight, water, chemical nutrients from the soil in order to survive. These are its values; these are what are good for it. Such ends are objective; they are a matter of hard fact;

they are not subject to whim or caprice; they are inalterably fixed by nature.

The same is true of animals. A lion, for example, must hunt in order to gain the meat its survival requires; without it, the beast perishes. The lion has no choice in this matter. Its values are set for it by nature.

Finally, human beings must grow food, construct dwellings, manufacture clothing, and cure disease. Their lives depend on it. To reach such achievements they must study agricultural science, architecture and engineering, biology, etc., and they must make the advances in philosophy, logic, and theoretical science that underlie such disciplines. Nature confronts man with a single, simple, pitiless alternative: cultivate the mind as a pre-condition to cultivate the soil—study, create, and grow—or die. Man, despite immeasurable intellectual advantages, is accorded no more choice by nature than any other organism. For him, as well, the alternative is stark: attain specific goals—or perish.

Fundamentally, there is a sole alternative in reality—existence or nonexistence; and it is faced exclusively by living beings. The sustained existence of inanimate matter does not require the satisfaction of conditions; matter simply is; it changes its forms ceaselessly, but it neither comes into nor goes out of existence. But life requires the attainment of certain ends. If an organism does not succeed in that endeavor, it perishes. Its material constituents endure—but its life is expunged. For example, the pulverizing of a rock and the pulverizing of a man are actions profoundly different in nature, in outcome, and in moral significance. The one merely changes its form—the other relinquishes its life.

Organic beings must reach specific goals in order to sustain their lives. It is because of this fundamental fact—and only because of it—that values come into existence. *Values are that which nature requires of an organism to maintain its life.* Rand states: "It is only the concept of 'Life' that makes the concept of 'Value' possible. It is only to a living entity that things can be good or evil."

Values are, therefore, grounded in fact; they are objective. It is reality—not society, or God, or an individual's own whim that necessitate plants gain water and sunlight, lions gain meat, and that human beings grow crops, build homes and cities, and cure diseases. Such matters are no more open to choice than is gravity. These are unyielding facts of nature.

The good for an organism is that which supports its life. The evil is that which harms or destroys it. For man, therefore, the standard of good and evil, the measuring rod by reference to which right and wrong are judged, is: the requirements of human life. *All that furthers man's earthly life is the good; all that inimical to it, is the evil.* Or, in another form: *for man, the good is all that which promotes the life of a rational being; the evil all that which harms or destroys it.*

Plants and animals automatically, inherently, and with no choice on their parts pursue the values that nature sets as a requirement to advance their lives. Plants cannot refuse to dig their roots into the soil—and hungry lions cannot eschew the hunt. Their instincts are not infallible and their knowledge is limited; when these prove inadequate, they perish. But as long as they are alive, they automatically pursue that which they sense as life-affirming, with no capacity to repudiate their interest and act as their own destroyers.

But because man is a rational being, he can understand moral principles and make moral choices. He can choose, for example, between nutritious food and poison—between education and ignorance—between individualism and bigotry—between productive work and parasitism off of honest men—between establishing a free society and imposing a dictatorship—between life-sustaining actions and those life-destroying.

Human beings do not automatically, intrinsically, nonvolitionally pursue that which advances their lives; they have the capacity to destroy themselves, to commit suicide in a multitude of forms—and quite often they do. They surrender their values to satisfy others—or they ingest toxic drugs—or they seek gain by deceitful conniving—or they vote for statist politicians—or in one of countless other modes sabotage their own lives and well-being.

Human beings must choose values, they must choose life, they must choose egoism.

It is a significant and immensely overlooked achievement to be an egoist—for it involves a scrupulous devotion to reality, to the survival requirements of human nature, and to positive, life-affirming values.

To be an egoist is to form, cherish, pursue, and never sacrifice life-advancing values.

Observe that only individuals are alive; regarding human life, only individual human beings live or die; indeed, at a deeper level, only particulars or entities—individual things—exist. The logical conclusion is that value achievement is a distinctively individual, personal pursuit.

In *The Fountainhead*, Howard Roark makes the important point that just as there is no collective stomach to digest food, so there is no collective brain to think. Digesting, thinking, breathing, and all other processes of body and mind are uniquely individualistic activities. Similarly—among human beings—there is no collective life form to seek or to gain values. Consequently, the possibility of value pursuit—and its necessity—is, utterly and exceptionlessly, an individualistic function.

Therefore, Rand states: "Man [each man] must live for his own sake, neither sacrificing himself to others nor sacrificing others to himself." To live for his own sake means that *the achievement of his own happiness is man's highest moral purpose.* Life is the *standard* of moral value, but his own happiness must be the *purpose* of each individual's life.

The necessity of individual value achievement in everyday life should be manifest. For example, a man must gain the education he needs; hold a productive job and earn wealth; seek close, trustworthy friends; and gain the intimacy of a romantic relationship—a set of values warranting fulfilled life, and a full absence of which precludes bare survival.

Granted that values are the means and the meaning of life, how—by what method—are they to be gained? In *Atlas Shrugged*, Rand provides a comprehensive answer. *The freethinking rational mind is the fundamental means by which human beings create values.*

Nature endows every species with some distinctive attribute by which to seek survival. For example, birds have wings to fly, lions claws and fangs with which to rend their prey, antelopes sufficient foot speed to outrun lions, elephants great size, gorillas immense strength, and many animals possess fur to keep them warm, etc.

These other species survive by physicalistic means—by strength, size, speed, etc. But man is, compared to many species, physically frail and unprepossessing. He cannot fly or outrun lions or overmatch gorillas in physical strength; and he is unadorned with fur to protect him from blizzard or freezing blast. Nature endows him with but one superlative characteristic by means of which to flourish—his intelligence.

Every value that human life depends on is a product of the reasoning mind. Food, for example, must be grown, entailing knowledge of agricultural science and invention of agricultural technology. Medicines must be researched and developed, requiring knowledge of biological science. Houses must be erected, necessitating knowledge of architecture, engineering, mathematics. All of these values, and thousands more, require thinking, understanding, and reasoning.

This is as true of the intellectual/spiritual values that further men's lives as it is of the material ones that do so. Whether it is Aristotle's advances in logic, or Newton's in theoretical science, or Edison's in applied science—or Shakespeare's achievements in literature, or Beethoven's in music, or Michelangelo's in sculpture, etc.—such creations are the product of genius, of the mind, of man's rational faculty. In *Atlas Shrugged*, Richard Halley, a brilliant composer, states:

> Whether it's a symphony or a coal mine, all work is an act of creating and comes from the same source: from an inviolate capacity to see through one's own eyes—which means: the capacity to perform a rational identification—which means: the capacity to see, to connect and to make what had not been seen, connected and made before. I...know what discipline, what effort, what tension of mind, what unrelenting strain upon one's power of clarity are needed to produce a work of art.

Rationality is man's survival instrument in the same literal sense that wings are a bird's.

This principle holds as true at an everyday level as on the grand scale. For example, a student gains knowledge by means of thinking; an auto mechanic identifies an engine's specific problem by means of thinking; a doctor diagnoses a patient's ailment by means of thinking; even a pizza delivery boy finds an unfamiliar street by reading a map and thinking. Interpersonal and international disputes are resolved without relapse into screaming irrationality and/or violent aggression—when and to the extent they are—by means of good faith negotiation, which involves a commitment to reasoning by all parties. An individual identifies serious character flaws in the man or woman he/she loves deeply only by an unbreached devotion to truth, including painful ones, which involves not emoting but thinking.

If man's life is the standard of the good, then that which sustains it—the reasoning mind—is a good without qualification.

No human characteristic is as selfish as an unbreached rationality—for it, above all, is responsible for the achievements, the creation of values, upon which human life depends.

Conversely, any repudiation of reason—any subordination of it to faith or feelings or supercilious authority—undermines man's survival instrument, his engine of creating values, his fundamental means of sustaining life.

If the sustenance of human life is the standard of the good, then evil lies in the rejection of the means by which human life is sustained.

Irrationality in any form renders value creation impossible. This is true regardless to which consideration reason is subordinated. Contemporary Islamists and the medieval Church reject(ed) reason for faith. The National Socialists (Nazis) eschewed it in favor of visceral gut reactions, what they felt in their "blood and bowels." The Communists paid lip service to science and reason, but, as philosophical materialists, denied the mind's efficacy, even its existence, and upheld manual labor—often whip-driven slave labor—as the source of all value production. All of these institutions and/or political theories—regardless of secondary differences—share a fundamental trait in common: they are evil, because they reject man's survival instrument. As a necessary consequence of such rejection, hundreds of millions did not survive, perishing (often by mass homicide) well before their times.

Human life requires production of values, not their destruction; creation of goods and services, not their plunder; rational thinking, not mindless brutality.

If human life is the standard of value, then *productivity is a major—and often neglected—moral virtue.* Every value human life requires—be it crops, computers, antibiotics, automobiles, apartment buildings, or one of a thousand others—must be produced by man's effort. Human beings, unlike the higher animals, do not discover readymade in nature the values their lives require. Man cannot long survive, much less prosper, by picking berries off a bush, hunting wild beasts with spears, and huddling in dank caves. He must cultivate crops, domesticate livestock, construct homes and cities, research and develop medications, invent electric light, the automobile, the airplane, the telephone, the computer, the Internet, etc.

Because the advancement of human life is the good, the creation of those values required by man's life forms the fundamental nature of a moral existence. Life-giving goods and services must be produced before they may be distributed—created before they may be given away. *It is the creation of life-supporting values, not their charitable re-distribution that is the preeminently virtuous act; for production is the driving engine of human survival.* Consequently, the great wealth creators of history—Andrew Carnegie, John D. Rockefeller, J.P. Morgan, Sam Walton, Bill Gates et al., are, qua productive giants, moral paragons; for such businessmen solved the problems of material production which plagued human life for millennia, enabling living standards to rise from bare subsistence to the historically unprecedented prosperity of the modern capitalist nations. Justice requires honest men to finally repudiate the egregiously mistaken "Robber Baron" view of such men and to honor them for their life-giving achievements.

If the creation of values urged by rational egoism is the essence of the good, what of the moral codes that oppose it? Fundamentally, in the history of moral philosophy, and, therefore, prevalent in human life, there are two such codes.

The first is *altruism*, the theory holding that virtue lies in self-sacrifice, in selfless service to others, whether the family, society, the state, the race, the proletariat, the tribe, etc. Need, to an altruist, constitutes an unchallengeable claim on a productive man's values; to the unending needs of others are sacrificed his effort, his achievements, his mind. "From each according to his ability," stated Karl Marx, "to each according to his need." Or as Rand succinctly explained altruism: "Whatever the value involved, it is your lack of it that gives you a claim to rewards."

The second is the theory endorsing a phony egoism—the basically devious view that the victimization of innocent others is both morally right and genuinely self-interested. This creed is best called: *cynical exploitativeness.*

Analyze them individually, starting with altruism.

Is it morally right for an individual to sacrifice those things and/or persons he most cherishes? To satisfy the needs of others, should he sacrifice his marriage, his children, his education, his career? The suffering and/or early death resulting from such value betrayal would be immense. Are such things legitimately demanded by a proper moral code? If not, what does sacrifice consist of? Should an individual give up only marginal elements of his life—mere moments of his time, a few dollars of his income, smidgens of his energy? Are such trifles genuinely *sacrifices*? If so, would not this utterly trivialize the creed of selflessness? Is it over such minutiae that the ethical dispute of the past two thousand years has been fought? Is this the version of selfless service to the state imposed on men by the Communists and National Socialists—or the version of selfless service to God levied by Islamists, Puritans, and the medieval Church?

If Bill Smith's need (or that of any man—or of society as a whole) imposes an unquestionable, undeniable moral duty on John Galt (or any honest man)—if Galt must serve Smith irrespective of Galt's preference or choice—then in what sense is Galt a free man? What became of his right to his own life, his own mind, his own choice? Altruism tramples individual freedom by elevating need above rights, and, consistently applied in political practice, leads necessarily to the full subjugation of the individual by the state.

If moral philosophers endorsed the probity of attaining life's important values, and exhorted "sacrifice" of only nonessentials, then they would be egoists, not altruists, and benignly undismayed by rational self-interest, personal gain, and profit-seeking. Some are precisely that, without even recognizing their own implicit egoism.

But there are those who are not benignly undismayed by rational self-interest; indeed, who are implacably hostile to it. In the cause of serving others—or the state—they exhort the sacrifice of personal values, and sanction (or at least tolerate) the massive suffering that inexorably results. For example, Kant, Hegel, Marx—a school of German philosophy dominating modern culture—urged, in varying forms, full-blown selflessness. The various forms of socialism emanating from this school put into political practice its moral code of selfless service to others, whether to the proletariat, the race, the state, etc. In the collectivist dictatorships of the twentieth century, the hideous results of this moral code consistently applied became manifest. This dreadful cancer in men's ethical lives—this creed of cadaverous death—was identified by Ayn Rand as the essence of "altruism," and, in attempt to excise this unlivable code and replace it with "the virtue of selfishness," she dedicated an immense amount of thought and writing.

Be clear that Objectivism does not equate helping others with sacrificing the self. The first is a significant good in human life; the second is an unqualified evil. If a man aids his friend, lover or spouse, or his child, it brings joy to help those important to him improve their station. Even helping a stranger brings a smile, a heartfelt "thank you," a sincere "you're welcome," and a moment of human contact. These are uniformly values, whether small, intermediate, or large.

But self-sacrifice, by definition, is the surrender or betrayal of values. Rand defined "sacrifice" as "the surrender of a greater value for a lesser value or a non-value." It is not a sacrifice if that which a man relinquishes is not a value to him—or a lesser one relative to the greater value he gains. So, for example, if a loving parent spends all of his money on his child's education and forgoes the new car he might have purchased, this is not a sacrifice, for the child means vastly more to him than the car; but if he spends all of his money to finance the education of strangers' children, and forgoes that of his child, it is.

Regarding the critical contrast between helping others and sacrificing the self: the one is life-promoting, and a consequent good; the other is life-harming, and a consequent evil. The former is to be actively pursued; the latter is to be strenuously opposed.

The second theory opposing rational egoism, cynical exploitativeness, although never fashionable among philosophers, lives a night-crawling existence in the blighted depths of human society. It consists of two interlocking premises: (1) It is to a man's actual self-interest to victimize innocent others and (2) it is morally right to do so. Both claims are inherently, abysmally, fatally false.

Rand wrote: "There is a fundamental moral difference between a man who sees his self-interest in production and a man who sees it in robbery." There absolutely is. A secondary, but still important difference lies in the social consequences, both for the individual himself and for others. The exploiter (or robber) harms others—while the producer benefits himself and others, as well. The producer, by creating wealth, can then exchange part of his output with other producers via voluntary trade that benefits all parties. But the cynical victimizer seeks, in effect, to live out a double standard: men must produce in order to survive—but he does not have to. He thereby makes enemies of society's most honest members; the best among mankind; those who choose to live out moral principles, to work productively, to create—not plunder—wealth, and to protect the innocent.

As a necessary result, he spends his life lying, sneaking, covering up the truth, attempting to hide his transgressions, on the run, a desperate man; in some cases, seeking escape from the police, who will put him in prison; in cases more extreme, from fellow scoundrels, who will put him in the ground; in all cases, from the rational discernment of honest men that will expose his tissue of deceit. This is a prescription for misery. Why embark on such a path to hell—when a world of shining values can be attained by rational productivity?

More fundamentally, the issue is not of a man's relationship to society—but to nature. Earth is not a Garden of Eden, where life-supporting values exist readymade for consumption. Such values, without exception, must be produced by human effort. Productive individuals live in harmony with this fact of reality; the parasite battles against it. It is a war no man can win. Society incarcerates him for theft—but nature expunges him when he runs out of victims.

Howard Roark stated the principle succinctly: "The creator's concern is the conquest of nature. The parasite's concern is the conquest of men." The producers create abundance and live well; they have no need of criminals or other parasites. But the parasites need them; like viruses, they survive only as leeches off of healthy beings; left to themselves—practicing their code in the absence of monumental change—they are incapable of bare survival. Understood in terms of such principles, it is apparent where an individual's rational self-interest lies.

For instance, how much food actually exists today, even in America, the world's wealthiest nation? If men decided to halt production—to cease growing, shipping, and selling food—and to instead subsist as parasites, how long would humanity endure? For, after the most cunning, violent brute robbed his final victim of the last morsel on earth, his own process of starvation inexorably ensues.

Rand wrote in *Atlas Shrugged*: "Man's life, as required by his nature, is not the life of a mindless brute, of a looting thug or a mooching mystic, but the life of a thinking being—not life by means of force or fraud, but life by means of achievement—not survival at any price, since there's only one price that pays for man's survival: reason."

What constitutes the deeper reason that cynical exploitativeness is not truly egoistic?

The theory urges gratification of personal desires—what Rand termed "whim worship"—as the essence of both selfishness and proper human conduct. (Included under this broad rubric is the narrower code of *hedonism*, which claims that bodily pleasure is the highest value in human life. So, for example, according to hedonism, toxic drugs are a value to a drug addict; liquor to an alcoholic; unrestrained sexuality to the promiscuous; etc.)

By claiming that gratification of personal desire is the *standard* of moral value, cynical exploitativeness—including its subtheme of hedonism—denies the factual basis of values; thereby leaving the code's practitioners no objective basis upon which to discriminate between life-supporting and life-destroying actions. In brief, the code is, in both its exploitativeness and its hedonism, self-destructive, not self-interested.

Altruism upholds the sacrifice of self to others. Cynical exploitativeness upholds the sacrifice of others to self. One code renders impossible the attainment of values by self; the other code renders impossible the attainment of values by the selves of others. Neither moral code has outgrown the primitive need of human sacrifice. The only difference between them regards who gets sacrificed to whom—whose values, personal happiness, and life itself is surrendered to whom.

The hero of *Atlas Shrugged* states perfectly the rational attitude toward sacrifice: "I swear by my life and my love of it that I will never live for the sake of another man, nor ask another man to live for mine." Philosopher Leonard Peikoff, Rand's leading student, wrote: "The principle embodied in this oath is that human sacrifice is evil no matter who its beneficiary is, whether you sacrifice yourself to others or others to yourself. Man—every man—is an end in himself." Egoism, properly understood, is a universal principle: the identical maxim that protects an individual from others protects others from the individual.

At the level of personal morality, the reasons explaining Rand's equation of the moral and the practical—and of the immoral and the impractical—can now be made clear.

Moral virtue lies in the creative, productive achievement of life-sustaining values. Similarly, practical success lies in the creative, productive achievement of life-sustaining values.

Immorality lies in opposition to the creative, productive achievement of life-sustaining values. Similarly, impracticality lies in opposition to the creative, productive achievement of life-sustaining values.

Men either create values and flourish—or, in some form, require sacrifice of values and thereby undermine their ability to flourish.

The question becomes: can value achievement be conducted equally well under all social systems—or does it require specific political–economic conditions? The answer, of course, is that political–economic freedom maximizes men's ability to create values—and that repression of such freedom minimizes or negates it.

If creation of values is the good, because man's life depends on it, then men must possess the moral right to create them. The fundamental right is, of course, the right to one's own life; which means, the right to produce and own values, and the right to deploy one's survival instrument—the mind—freely in the production of values. Each man's moral right to his own life must be protected.

Rand points out that only other men can abrogate an individual's right to his own life—*and only by the initiation of force against him.*

The use of rational persuasion in attempt to convince a man to surrender his values still leaves him free to choose between the alternative of self-fulfillment or self-sacrifice. But not so with the brutes who initiate force against him. A robber who steals a man's wealth—or an assailant who assaults his body—or a dictator who forces him into a gulag, etc., leave him with no such alternative; against his will, they expunge his life or diminish it.

In effect, they assault not merely his body, but his mind. Although the brute cannot literally thrust his hands into an individual's mind and compel it to comply with his demands, a force initiator nevertheless makes the victim's thinking irrelevant to his actions; for left free, the victim would choose neither to surrender his wealth to the thief nor his life to the murderer. The initiation of force—or the threat of it—negates a man's ability to act on the judgment of his mind; *negates his ability to act in accordance with his instrument of survival—and, consequently, in principle, leaves him no means of survival.*

Men need protection from the initiation of force against them. Their ability to attain values depends on it; their ability to deploy their survival instrument depends on it; their ability to survive depends on it. Their ability to achieve the good depends on it.

The initiation of force must be universally banned from human life.

This moral principle cannot be sufficiently emphasized: All forms of the initiation of force, including fraud, its indirect use, must be excised from human life.

This is why human beings need a government. A proper government recognizes and protects the principle of individual rights—of an individual's right to his own life, to the pursuit of the values that sustain it, and to the independent employment of his instrument of survival.

This was the moral revolution embodied in the founding of the American Republic. Whatever the nation's flaws, its founding principles made it the freest, the greatest, the most moral nation of history. The U.S. Constitution and Bill of Rights were a noble attempt to ban—or, at least, severely curtail—the initiation of force against innocent men. In effect, the government protected men from private criminals—and the Constitution and Bill of Rights protected men from the government.

The American system was imperfect. In numerous forms, it permitted the violation of individual rights: slavery, of course, was an egregious abrogation of the country's basic founding principles—and, later, legally imposed racial segregation continued governmental initiation of force against black (and white) Americans. Further, such policies as eminent domain, a military draft, confiscatory taxation, the coercive redistribution of wealth, the regulation of productive businesses, prohibition of alcohol and other drugs, a legal ban on gay marriage, and numerous other laws made the United States not a fully free country—but a mixed system, combining extensive elements of governmental protection of individual rights with a growing element of the state's violation of such rights. Today's mixed economy—as fully real in the world's other semi-capitalist nations as in America—is a curious anomaly, where, regarding some issues the government protects innocent men from the initiation of force, while, regarding others, it itself initiates force against the same individuals.

Nevertheless, the foundation of the American Republic initiated a moral revolution. In proclaiming that an individual has the inalienable right to life, liberty, and the pursuit of happiness—in legally protecting a man's freedom of speech, of the press, of intellectual expression—in similarly upholding his freedom of religion, his right to own property, to start a business and earn and retain wealth, and his right to bear arms—the United States became a historically important nation: the country where individual rights were more widely recognized, respected, and protected by its government than at any time before, anywhere on earth.

Rand (herself an immigrant to the United States from the Soviet Union) stated: "*America's founding ideal was the principle of individual rights...* The rest—everything that America achieved, everything she became, every thing 'noble and just,' and heroic, and great, and un-precedented in human history—was the logical consequence of fidelity to that one principle." This principle constitutes the defining essence of the capitalist system that Rand so eloquently defended. "Capital-ism," she wrote, "is the system of individual rights, including property rights, in which all property is privately owned."

The United States was the nation where the legal initiation of force against innocent men was at a historic, all-time low.

This was especially true during the late-nineteenth and turn-of-the-twentieth centuries—and especially in the northern states. The 13th Amendment ended slavery in 1865, although, in the south, the Jim Crow era was just beginning. But in the north, for roughly forty years, until the so-called "Progressive Era" accelerated government's initiation of force against productive businesses, the United States enjoyed the system that was the closest the world has yet come to one of unfettered, laissez-faire capitalism. The principle of individual rights protected the best among mankind: those who chose to think—to consistently deploy their survival instrument in the creation of life-supporting values.

The free-thinking mind, the fundamental source of new ideas and creations in every field, is stifled under all forms of statism. The thinkers must bow to the King or the Church or Hitler or Stalin or the Taliban or the Ayatollahs et al. Their thinking is proscribed within the rigid boundaries defined by the state—and if they dare transgress those boundaries, they are confronted by the prospect of the rack or the stake or the gulag. In the absence of a legally protected principle of individual rights, a man's life belongs to the state; and *if his life so belongs, so, necessarily, does his mind.* Thinking is curtailed. Progress halts. Regress often ensues. Abysmal poverty is the norm.

The freer a country, the more protected are its thinkers. The more stringently a ban on the initiation of force is practiced by a nation's government, the more the creators of life-giving wealth will flourish. And the freest countries will flourish the most.

Late-nineteenth and turn-of-the-twentieth-century America provide abundant evidence supporting these claims. The leading thinkers of American culture—free to express any idea; to write any book; to invent new technologies; to originate companies; to compete with older ideas or technologies; to showcase the new ideas/products to the consumers; to, in time, win them to the cause of progress—stunned the world with an outpouring of genius in every field. These were advances so stunning that today, a century later, they are still undetected by punch drunk, anticapitalist historians, who continue to deride the era as "the Gilded Age"; but which were and remain widely detected by the "common man" worldwide, who then and now sought to flock to America to partake of its unprecedented freedom and its consequent unprecedented intellectual and material prosperity.

The outpouring of genius included Samuel Morse and the creation of the telegraph (slightly earlier in the nineteenth century); Thomas Edison and the invention of an electric lighting system; Alexander Graham Bell and the creation of the telephone; William LeBaron Jenney and Louis Sullivan and the pioneering of skyscrapers, first in Chicago, later in New York and elsewhere; John Roebling and the perfection of the suspension bridge, and construction of his masterpiece, the Brooklyn Bridge, still carrying thousands of cars and trucks daily, some 125 years later; Henry Ford and the mass production of automobiles; the Wright brothers and the development of aviation; George Eastman and the revolutionizing of photography; George Westinghouse and Nikola Tesla and development of an AC induction motor capable of generating electricity safely across vast distances; Cyrus Field and the laying of a transatlantic cable, making possible virtually instant communication between North America and Europe; and thousands of other innovators and the progress they wrought. Even in the Jim Crow south, George Washington Carver was left sufficiently free at Tuskegee Institute (by a racist state government that could not bother to concern itself with the goings-on at black schools) to revolutionize the field of agricultural science; and rational men—individualists, consequently nonbigots—across the nation of liberty were free to recognize, honor, and apply Carver's advances.

Even eminent American historian, Charles Beard, generally no friend to free markets, wrote regarding the years between 1865 and 1900: "Nearly every year between the close of the civil conflict and the end of the century witnessed some signal achievement in the field of applied science."

Further, in business, industry, and banking, this era in American history showed unprecedented progress. Andrew Carnegie, for example, pioneered the mass production of steel, dramatically improving its quality and lowering its cost, thereby making affordable the construction of skyscrapers, of automobiles, of transcontinental railroads and subway systems, of farm equipment, and of much more. Similarly, John D. Rockefeller, refined copious quantities of oil, also dramatically reducing its price, lighting American homes with kerosene lamps, not candles, producing inexpensive gasoline that enabled Henry Ford to revolutionize personal transportation in America, and permitting millions of Americans to heat their homes and cook their food more cheaply than ever before. Great railroad men like James J. Hill and Edward H. Harriman built productive transcontinental railroads (or re-constructed into productive lines inefficient, already-existing ones), consistently lowering freight rates, making it cheaper for producers to ship goods to market, thereby lowering costs for consumers. The brilliant financier, J.P. Morgan, funded numerous productive enterprises, including Hill's and Edison's experiments with electric light; successfully re-organized a number of foundering railroads; and not once but twice saved the country from financial disaster in response to the urgent pleas of the U.S. Government.

Prominent American historian, Louis Hacker, wrote in his book, *The World of Andrew Carnegie 1865–1901:* "The 'Robber Barons' were not the despoilers we have been led to believe. The United States of the post-Civil War period...was transformed in not more than a single generation into the greatest industrial nation of the world...A complete transportation net, the beginnings of the generation of electrical power...the creation of new industries, the modernization of farm plant: all these were accomplished in this brief time. *In consequence all sectors of the economy benefited.*" (Emphasis added.)

During this era, American production of petroleum rose by greater than 9,000 percent; of steel by greater than 10,000 percent. Real wages—income measured in terms of purchasing power, of what customers can buy with their money—rose by 20 percent. Per capita income grew by an average of roughly 3 percent annually. National wealth displayed a fourfold increase, from $30 billion to greater than $120 billion. Economist, Jonathan Hughes, in his book, *The Vital Few*, writing of this period, stated: "This rise in population, enormous as it was, was actually outstripped by increases in output of goods and services to such an extent that the rising output per head of population came to be a thing taken for granted by Americans."

Additionally, predictably, the Humanities flourished in the nation that most fully protected freethinkers from the initiation of force. For example, throughout the 1880s, William James pioneered the discipline of experimental psychology by operating the world's first research laboratory in the field at Harvard University; in 1890, publishing his massive, two-volume, brilliantly groundbreaking, *The Principles of Psychology.* Despite its relative youth as a country, America produced a body of national literature second to none, boasting such luminaries as Nathaniel Hawthorne, Edgar Allan Poe, Herman Melville, Walt Whitman, Mark Twain, and continuing in the twentieth century with Ernest Hemingway, William Faulkner, F. Scott Fitzgerald, and the still under-appreciated Russian immigrant, Ayn Rand. The latter, utterly out of the intellectual mainstream, wrought not merely several brilliant novels but revolutionized the field of philosophy, a truth that only now, almost thirty years after her death, is beginning to be acknowledged by academic philosophers. In America, Rand had only to deal with calumny and neglect, not the secret police, slave labor camps, and mass murders of her native Russia during the Soviet era.

Also under the freedom of the American system, a mass publishing industry was created, centered in New York City and its environs. In the decades following Edison's 1877 invention of the phonograph, a mass music industry gradually developed, largely in America. The film industry was born in America, centered now for almost a century in Hollywood. Opera companies, ballet troupes, and art museums flourish in every major city; and thousands of colleges and universities

21

proudly offer multiple philosophy courses, where any ideas may be freely expressed and/or challenged.

The intellectual and material wealth necessary to support human life are products of the mind—and the mind requires political–economic freedom to function independently, to think outside the parameters of society's cherished mores, and to thereby create new theories and devices.

By contrast, under statism in any of its ghastly iterations—be it theocracy, military dictatorship, National Socialism, Communism, etc.—the state has the legal authority to initiate force against innocent men at any time under any pretext. *For if an individual's life belongs to the state, then no moral principle constrains the state from disposing of each life as it deems best.* In the absence of protecting individual rights as a moral principle forming the bedrock foundation of a government's purpose, such bloody tyrants as Hitler, Stalin, Mao, Pol Pot et al., inexorably rise to power, and are ethically unrestrained from exterminating extensive portions of their country's population (in the case of Pol Pot and the Khmer Rouge, a staggering 25 percent of Cambodia's entire population was slaughtered in the four years between 1975 and 1979).

Related, such a morally unconstrained regime can and will and does incarcerate and/or execute freethinkers who challenge its decrees; it can and will and does burn books, impose censorship, and flood its schools with propaganda rather than knowledge; forming a complex of repressive policies that lead inevitably to regression and precipitous decline into Dark Age or abysmal collapse. The medieval Christians, for example, by burning "heretics" at the stake (i.e., independent minds who dared challenge the Church's orthodoxy), by closing the illustrious Greek centers of learning, by refusing to permit pagans—despite often great levels of knowledge—to teach, and by burning manuscripts, was a leading cause of the infamous Dark Age of the fifth to the ninth centuries. The repression and murder of intellectual dissidents in Soviet Russia made it impossible for that country to keep pace with America's growth, in economic terms or any other, and led inevitably to destitution, shameless dependence on the semi-capitalist West, and ignominious crumbling. The incalculable repression of North Korea makes it impossible, despite immense brain power of the country's population, to rise even millimeters above a level of collapse.

Worse, statism also constitutes the root cause of mankind's interminably bloody warfare.

For if a government embodies no principled commitment to uphold and protect the rights and lives of its own citizens, what moral precept guides it to respect the rights and lives of foreigners? None.

Observe that it was the two murderous dictatorships—National Socialist Germany and Soviet Russia—that, as allies, invaded Poland in September 1939, thereby precipitating World War II. It was not semi-free Britain, France, or America that plunged the world into the bloodiest conflict of history. Further, it was Communist North Korea that, with Stalin's blessing, invaded freer South Korea, not vice versa. Similarly, it was Communist North Vietnam that successfully sought to conquer the freer South Vietnam; it was not from the corrupt (but vastly less authoritarian) South Vietnamese Government or its American allies that millions of Vietnamese "boat people" fled for their lives; understandably, it was from the Communists. It was the armies of Saddam Hussein that conquered Kuwait, not freer and wealthier Kuwait that organized armies to conquer Iraq. It was only after decades of bloody terrorist assaults on her, culminating in the atrocities of 9/11, that America roused sufficiently to defend itself; and even then left the primary engine of Islamist terrorism—the Iranian regime—utterly unscathed.

Statism is the fundamental cause of war.

The internecine warfare of mankind's long, often inglorious history has extinguished untold billions of human lives—how many of them potential Aristotle's, Newton's, Michelangelo's, Shakespeare's, Mozart's et al., can never be determined. It has leveled cities and towns, destroyed fertile fields, and eradicated wealth-creating factories and businesses. It has kept men fighting and dying, rather than working productively. It is vastly easier to discern the created rather than the uncreated; for the one stares a man in the face, while the other does not yet exist. The intellectual and material advances not created because of the interminable savagery is literally incalculable; but there is no doubt that mankind is immeasurably poorer for it.

The denial of individual rights in the form of statism, or the closely related theory of *collectivism*—the dominance of the group over the individual; and the subordination of the individual to a "higher" authority, whether the State or the Race or the Tribe or the Community of Religious Believers or another, is the cause of every atrocity committed in human politics, whether it be slavery or genocide or imperialism or jihadist terrorism or any other.

23

The initiation of force must be universally banned from human life; especially on the part of the government, the social institution charged with responsibility for protecting men from it. A statist regime is vastly more dangerous than a private gangster, for the thug struggles against the power of the criminal justice system, which protects the innocent, whereas a government embodies the criminal justice system and holds a legal monopoly on the use of force in a given geographic area; consequently, its victims have no legal recourse against it. A dictator controls the nation's military, the police, the courts, the prisons, etc. This is why a Hitler or a Mao—but not an Al Capone or a John Gotti—can exterminate *tens of millions* of innocent victims.

Again, this time at the political level, Rand's reasons for equating the moral and the practical—and the immoral and the impractical—become apparent.

The moral is to protect individual rights. Similarly, the practical is to protect individual rights.

The moral is to uphold the right of every individual to employ his survival instrument in the quest to create values. Similarly, the practical is to uphold the right of every individual to employ his survival instrument in the quest to create values.

The moral is to sedulously ban the initiation of force from every aspect of human life. Similarly, the practical is to sedulously ban the initiation of force from every aspect of human life.

What advances human life *is the good.* It follows that *what advances human life* is the good.

The converse is also necessarily true.

The immoral is to abrogate individual rights. Similarly, the impractical is to abrogate individual rights.

The immoral is to violate the right of any individual to employ his survival instrument in the quest to create values. Similarly, the impractical is to violate the right of any individual to employ his survival instrument in the quest to create values.

The immoral is to initiate force. Similarly, the impractical is to initiate force.

Rand's equation of the moral with the practical will be a central explanatory principle employed in this book in the attempt to satisfactorily resolve America's most intractable contemporary dilemmas.

There is a final point—a deeper philosophical issue—that will also be of importance in understanding America's current challenges;

especially regarding environmentalism and its claim of man-made global warming. This is the key idea from which Rand derived the name of her philosophic system: her theory of objectivity.

Objectivity is both a *metaphysical* and an *epistemological* principle.

(Metaphysics is the branch of philosophy that studies the nature of the universe taken as a totality, of those characteristics that apply to all things, not merely a subset of them, e.g., what the universe is composed of, whether it is eternal or created, etc. Epistemology is the branch of philosophy that studies the means by which men gain knowledge of life's important truths, e.g., whether by observation-based rationality or by faith or by regarding their feelings as self-certifying absolutes, etc.)

Metaphysically, Rand upheld the primacy of facts—that existence is, facts are what they are, and that reality cannot be altered by the mere wish or desire of any mind or consciousness, whether animal, human, or divine, if such a consciousness existed.

Contrast, for a moment, Rand's conviction of the absolutism of facts with a differing view dominant in the modern world—that society is omnipotent, and that, in some form, can bend reality to its will. For example, according to historian, Paul Johnson, in his book, *Modern Times*, Chinese Communist dictator, Mao Tse-tung, "did not believe in 'objective situations' at all." Rather, he believed in the power of man's will to subordinate reality to itself. Presumably, on his view, the Chinese people—if they willed it with sufficient force—could fly across the Pacific simply by flapping their arms.

Certainly Pol Pot and the Khmer Rouge (the Cambodian Communists) held a similar view. They believed that if the proletariat willed it, jungle terrain could be converted into fertile agricultural lands, despite the soil's unsuitability; this attempt to defy reality was, of course, a disaster.

Rand's view, in contrast to these others, was best summed up in Bacon's famous aphorism: "Nature, to be commanded, must be obeyed." The laws of nature are immutable.

Epistemologically, it follows from the absolutism of facts that knowledge requires men's thinking to adhere scrupulously to them. This is not an automatic process. Since man is a fallible being, he can err regarding all manner of conclusions, including important ones, no matter the punctilious honesty of his character. Worse, human beings can choose irrationality—to place an arbitrary desire or whim

25

above and before facts they find unpleasant. To gain knowledge, to ascertain truth human beings must voluntarily initiate and sustain a reality-based method of thought. Man gains knowledge by certain means—reason—adhering to specific rules—logic.

Aristotle formulated the rules of proper reasoning long ago; in the modern world, Rand ascertained the essence of the field: *logic is the art of non-contradictory identification.*

There are three central principles at the heart of Aristotle's ground-breaking advances in logic. The first is the Law of Identity, rendered schematically as "A is A"—a thing is what it is. The second is the Law of Non-Contradiction—or: "A is not non-A"—a thing is not what it is not. The last is the Law of Excluded Middle—or: A thing cannot be both A and non-A at the same time and in the same respect; in other words, critically, contradictions do not and cannot exist.

Contradictions exist only in the thinking of muddled minds; there are none in reality. To maintain a contradiction is to commit the fundamental error of reasoning. To arrive at a contradiction, Rand maintained, is to acknowledge an error in one's reasoning. "To maintain a contradiction is to abdicate one's mind and to evict oneself from the realm of reality."

The principle of noncontradiction is the ruling axiom of rational cognition. Leonard Peikoff wrote: "Whenever one moves by a volitional process from known data to a new cognition ostensibly based on these data, the ruling question must be: can the new cognition be integrated *without contradiction* into the sum of one's knowledge?"

Such noncontradictory integration is the essence of objectivity.

For example, the theory of evolution is still disputed by some religionists. The theory claims that all life forms on earth—including man, the most biologically sophisticated—developed over time from a single common ancestor. Does this idea integrate with what we know about life and about the earth? Research shows that it does indeed fit seamlessly into an extensive range of knowledge.

Geologists, for instance, estimate the earth's age at roughly 4.5 billion years. Fossil records show life forms dating back to 3.5 billion years ago. In keeping with the theory that more complex life forms developed from simpler ones, the earliest fossil records are of bacteria. In keeping with the theory that life arose naturally from what paleontologist Niles Eldredge terms "pre-biotic chemical constituents," rocks that are 3.8 billion years old show "forms of carbon atoms (isotopes) considered by bio-chemists as a fingerprint of the presence of life."

Fossil records show that for one billion years, life forms on earth were restricted to bacteria. Fossils also show that the earliest forms of animal life appeared roughly 535 million years in the past—and that the human lineage appeared only some four million years ago. There exists a gradation of "fossil human remains spanning the duration of the last three million years in Africa"—showing a steady, continuous development from apelike creatures to modern man.

Further, advances in genetic science reveal the same RNA and DNA structure in all living forms—bacteria, fungi, plants, animals, man—powerful evidence for the claim of an interconnected line of biological descent.

The theory of evolution integrates without contradiction a vast sum of empirical data identified by scientists in a wide range of fields—geology, paleontology, biochemistry, and genetics, to name only a few.

Additionally, its cognitive method is fact-based and naturalistic, making no transcendent references in the attempt to explain the genesis of human life; it thereby integrates with the central philosophic truth that reason—not faith, feelings, or any similarly irrational "method"—is man's means of gaining knowledge and guiding successful life.

Is there any knowledge—any hard factual data—that contradicts the claims of evolution? None. All that opposes it is the explicitly faith-based claim of creationism—or its modern camouflaged version, the theory of intelligent design.

(Afterall, the claim that the sophistication of earth's life forms (or of the universe itself) argues for an intelligent designer surely applies equally to the designer. Such a designer would be a creative genius, whose complexity, on this theory, would count as evidence that he or it was designed. By whom? An illogical infinite regress of designers is then required. It is the identical illogic spawned by faith-based systems. For if earth can only be explained by postulating a Creator, how does the Creator escape such requirements? Who or what created the Creator?)

The theory of evolution is thereby established by reference to the broad range of scientific and philosophic knowledge with which it coheres without contradiction. It forms a seamless part of an integrated rational view of existence.

Objectivity as a method of acquiring knowledge entails the unified, noncontradictory integration of an idea or theory into the broadest range of knowledge possible.

This brief account of Objectivism is not a systematic presentation of the entire philosophic system (for that the reader is referred to this author's *Objectivism in One Lesson*—and to Leonard Peikoff's advanced text, *Objectivism the Philosophy of Ayn Rand*). It is simply the minimum amount of philosophy necessary to provide rational solutions to America's current ethical and political problems.

Part Two:
Rational Solutions to
Current Moral/Political
Problems

1

Repudiating Environmentalism in Theory and Practice

The United States, history's most scientifically and technologically advanced nation, is threatened with an energy shortage. The country whose innovative thinkers pioneered the oil industry must today go begging for oil to sundry Third World dictators who hate America. One result is that American customers face greatly higher prices for gasoline and other petroleum products, which significantly diminish their living standards. Why?

Because environmentalist polices have strangled American energy producers.

For decades, energy companies have been prevented from creating new oil refineries, from drilling offshore on the Outer Continental Shelf (OCS), and from exploiting oil in the Arctic National Wildlife Refuge (ANWR). For example, no new American oil refineries have been constructed since the 1970s. Since 1990, federal bans have prevented the U.S. companies from producing America's enormous offshore energy resources; a full 97% of America's two billion acres of lands on the OCS are not exploited for their energy potential. Similarly, for decades, oil companies have not been permitted to develop the huge supply of petroleum in ANWR's remote coastal plain. The inexorable economic result is a shortage of energy in the country and rising prices for consumers.

Fossil fuels, say the greens, leave a huge "carbon footprint" and contribute to both environmental degradation and the looming catastrophe of global warming. Their current "solution" is proposed "cap and trade" legislation, a nightmare piece of insanity that might have proceeded straight from the pages of *Atlas Shrugged.*

Cap and trade imposes a national limit (cap) on all carbon emissions. Companies are then allocated a specific number of permits to emit such gases, permits that they must purchase, and which they are then permitted to sell on the marketplace (trade). The national limit is reduced each year in an attempt to reduce carbon emissions below a certain level.

The horror of such a proposal is manifest. Morally, it violates the rights of productive businessmen by forcing them to purchase permits to deploy oil, natural gas, or coal to fuel manufacturing. Related, it inevitably spawns massive corruption, for it creates a noxious breeding ground for "pull peddlers." These are businessmen who gain wealth not by superb productivity on a free market but by currying favor with federal regulators and legislators in a marketplace partially controlled by government. Such businessmen with powerful "friends" in DC somehow procure permits more readily than those who have none—and increase their profit by selling them to producers desperate to stave off bankruptcy but lacking friends in Washington. In *Atlas Shrugged*, James Taggart is such a blood-sucking creature; in real life, unfortunately, General Electric, in part, has morphed into one.

Such corruption is often referred to as "crony capitalism," but since it is made possible only by significant government control of the marketplace, it is fitting to call it by its proper name: "half-assed socialism." (Full socialism is the totalitarianism of Communism and National Socialism—or Nazism.)

Practically, the harm to the U.S. economy will be colossal. Such a policy amounts to a tax on the use of major energy sources. The increased expense of buying the right to use fuel will put out of business marginal producers. Other firms will be forced to scale back production. Output will correspondingly decline, so a diminishing supply of goods and services relative to demand for them means higher prices for customers. Declining output ensures inevitably rising unemployment. (A year after imposing its own cap and trade program, Spain currently experiences 18% unemployment.) As time goes on, the ceiling on emissions is to be steadily reduced, so fewer permits are made available (except, of course, to pull peddlers); their price rises, the cost of production thereby increases, and the downward cycle intensifies.

On some estimates, manufacturing jobs are expected to decline by an average of four hundred thousand per year between 2012 and 2035. American agriculture, employing natural-gas-derived fertilizer and relying heavily on fossil fuels, will suffer immensely. Prohibitively high fuel costs, as elsewhere in the economy, will cause decreased production, diminished supply, and much higher food prices. Further, household energy costs are estimated to rise 29% above current levels, even though customers will have switched to smaller cars, moved into energy-efficient homes, use more public transportation, etc.

Americans, enjoying the world's highest standard of living, will begin the plunge toward the diminished living standards of European-style semi-socialism—and much lower if environmentalists have their way.

Americans do not have to tolerate this. Indeed, emphatically, they should not.

Here is what must be done:

Cap and trade must be utterly, categorically repudiated. Any similar proposal to limit carbon emissions by coercive governmental decree must be soundly rejected. Freedom must be restored in the field of energy production. ANWR should be opened to drilling by American energy producers; the same regarding the OCS. America's extensive natural gas supply should be fully developed. The right of power companies to once again construct nuclear plants must be legally upheld; the same is true of the right to build new oil refineries. The ruling principle is: environmentalist bans on production of domestic energy sources must be fully repealed.

America's mottoes must be variations on the old truth that "Bigger is Better." The contemporary versions should be: "Create More, Consume More"—or "Produce More, Own More."

The moral virtue of such freedom is that the inalienable right of productive men to create wealth is stringently upheld—and the government's coercive power to abrogate such rights is legally curtailed. The practical benefit lies in an over-brimming supply of fuel that will vastly lower prices, greatly increase American living standards, and advance productivity and research in a plethora of fields.

Why have Americans permitted themselves to be shackled? Why have we strangled domestic production of energy and natural resources and crippled our own economy? Why have the freest, most enterprising people of history permitted its government to violate the rights of energy producers and other creative men? From whence does this rights-violating, economy-crushing insanity proceed?

From the intellectual cesspool that is environmentalism.

If America is to re-establish itself as a free country, and re-assert itself as an energy-rich economic powerhouse, every error and popular canard of this virulent philosophy must be identified, exposed, and refuted.

Today, and for recent decades, millions of people regard(ed) environmentalism as a benign force, a "sort of global sanitation department," in Peter Schwartz's ironic phrase; a movement determined to cleanse the earth's air and water of toxic pollutants.

This is a tragically superficial and largely false appraisal. Intellectual–moral–political movements are often eclectic mixtures of diverse elements; and although possible that many rank-and-file members of the eco-crusade genuinely believe its mission is to expunge pollutants in service of human life, the intellectual–political leadership of environmentalism emphatically does not. In fact, the shoddy secret necessary to understand environmentalism's essence is its relentlessly implacable hostility to human life. Mankind's noblest and freest periods—e.g., Classical Athens, Renaissance Italy, the eighteenth-century Western Enlightenment, and nineteenth-century America—have been actuated by a philosophy of *Humanism*, the recognition that human life and its advancement is the highest moral value. By contrast, environmentalism must be identified as an *anti-Humanist* movement.

The evidence supporting this assessment is overwhelming. In case after endless case, virtually without exception, environmentalists deny human values—including life-saving ones—in favor of the nonhuman. A case in point is green opposition to development of oil on the coastal plain of the ANWR. To be kind, this part of ANWR, in Alaska's far northern reaches, is forsaken wilderness—brutally cold during winter's interminable months, a mosquito-infested hellhole by summer. But it contains oil—lots and lots of oil—according to geologists, over seven billion barrels worth. Such supply could reduce America's dependency on oil produced by hostile dictatorships, lower the price for petroleum products, including gasoline, and raise American living standards, especially that of the working poor, who generally are unable to work from home. But according to environmentalists it is pristine wilderness—therefore sacred—and habitat to the cherished caribou. Human living standards are to be sacrificed to remote wilderness and reindeer herds.

The truth is even worse. The small wilderness area in which drilling would occur is neither majestic mountain range nor spacious ocean vista—but flat, dreary tundra—full night, lacking a hint of sunlight during winter months, and swept by near-one hundred-degree-below-zero wind chill; by summer, miles of pock-marked coastal plain, punctured by huge puddles from melting ice that breed swarms of pestilential flying insects. It is, consequently, the nation's sole region identified by the U.S. Government as both swamp and desert. During the 1980s, *The Washington Post* aptly observed: "[T]hat part of the [ANWR] is one of the bleakest, most remote places on this continent..."

Further, the Central Arctic caribou herd has flourished since construction of the earlier Alaskan Pipeline, increasing in number five-fold over its duration; for one thing, the animals snuggle up to or under the piping for warmth during Alaska's withering winter. The new technology of directional drilling, which can drill down hundreds of feet, then sideways for miles, then upward, is scarcely invasive on the barren landscape—and, finally, the Inupiat Eskimos, who inhabit the coastal plain, overwhelmingly favor drilling, for the revenues they will receive will raise their subsistence living standards.

None of these truths matter to the environmentalists—but must be remembered, for they constitute evidence of a virulent anti-man bias.

Perhaps more telling was the 1990s controversy regarding taxol, derived from the Pacific yew tree, and, at the time, considered an effective medicine in mankind's struggle against cancer. The head of the National Cancer Institute stated that taxol was "the most important new drug we have had in cancer in fifteen years." But because the yew trees were considered scarce and were home to the spotted owl, environmentalists were against their use. Al Gore, in his book, *Earth in the Balance*, wrote: "It seems an easy choice—sacrifice the tree for a human life—until one learns that three trees must be destroyed for each patient treated...Suddenly we must confront some tough questions." So it is a difficult moral choice between human lives and those of trees and owls? Bear in mind also that pacific yew trees, when cut down, can and would be replanted in droves.

Further, decades ago the Environmental Protection Agency (EPA) banned the use of DDT, a restriction continuing to this day, although its own research established that the substance was harmless to human and animal life, but lethal to malaria-carrying mosquitoes. By the 1970s, mankind had succeeded in virtually expunging the scourge of malaria—but since the DDT prohibition, the disease has made a deadly comeback; indeed, each year hundreds of thousands of human beings (perhaps more) are again killed by it, largely in impoverished Asian and African countries. Human life is sacrificed to that of mosquitoes.

35

Related, the environmentalists' intellectual/moral brethren in the animal rights movement oppose medical research on laboratory mice, even though such methods were instrumental in winning the battles against polio and diabetes, and are similarly necessary for inquiry seeking cures for heart disease, AIDS, and other fatal human illnesses. Human life is sacrificed to that of rodents.

Some people are willing to overlook or, at least, minimize such insanities on the grounds that at least the environmentalists have succeeded in cleaning earth's air and water—or intend to—a value that is authentically beneficial to human life. What is the truth concerning this?

The current popularity of the preposterous notion that technology and industrialization pollute the environment in no way minimizes its standing as a lethal canard. For example, in pre-industrial societies the predominant, agonizing public health question is: How to keep human and animal excrement out of the drinking water? The terrible answer is: It is impossible. The tragic consequences are the appallingly high death rates from cholera, diphtheria, typhus, and other diseases caused by water-borne toxins—and the severely reduced life expectancies that ensue. Such calamities are averted solely by invention and mass production of inexpensive steel, construction of sealed, leak-proof water and sewer mains, chlorination of water, and the erection of vast networks of reservoirs supplying clean water to every home and building across the breadth of a continent.

Further, such environmental cleansing entails modern methods of sewerage treatment and disposal—and, similarly, of garbage. This requires prodigious advance in theoretical and applied science, engineering, technology, and industrialization. In the absence of such—in medieval Europe, for example—human excrement and garbage was simply dumped in river or stream; dead animals might lie in the road for days; rats, fleas, lice, and other vermin infested inhabited areas; and virulent disease was unabatedly rampant—including bubonic plague, which, carried by the fleas of rats, in the mid-fourteenth century expunged tens of millions of human lives in roughly three to four years in Western Europe alone.

On a related point, at the time that the Clean Air Act was passed in 1970, America's air was becoming progressively cleaner, not dirtier, and had been doing so for decades. Measurements in fourteen U.S. cities in 1931–32 showed an average particulate concentration of 510 micrograms per cubic meter. By 1957, it was down to 120 micrograms per cubic meter—and by 1969, the measurement stood at 92 micrograms per cubic meter. The major reason for this positive trend was conversion to such cleaner burning fuels as oil, gas, and nuclear, away from coal or wood. Improvements in technology on a free market caused this trend, not environmentalist propaganda or governmental legislation.

It is worth noting that environmentalists have long opposed development of nuclear power, and have, via endless and cost-incurring litigation, stymied for decades the ability of American power companies to erect plants driven by this cleanest of energy sources. Remember that, today, in 2011, France generates roughly 75% of its electricity by means of nuclear power—and that, for fifty years the U.S. Navy has safely deployed nuclear-driven submarines and surface vessels. The worst nuclear "accident" in U.S. history—at Three Mile Island (TMI) in 1979—harmed zero human lives.

Nuclear power is by far the safest, cleanest form of large-scale energy conversion currently available. Because it employs a miniscule fraction of the fuel required by fossil-fired plants (those using coal, oil, or gas) far fewer deaths occur from mining or railroad accidents or from the horrific "Black Lung Disease," widespread among coal miners. Because fossil plants pump toxic pollutants into the atmosphere, a one thousand-megawatt plant of such type causes an estimated seventy deaths per year; because nuclear plants pour out no such pollutants, and because the amount of radiation emitted is extraordinarily low when compared to that absorbed daily from natural sources, a nuclear plant causes zero deaths via emission.

The case for nuclear power's superiority to fossil plants regarding safety and pollution can be established on every issue, including (and especially)waste disposal, and has been brilliantly set forth by professor of electrical engineering, Petr Beckmann, in his book, *The Health Hazards of NOT Going Nuclear.* In the capitalist or semi-capitalist nations, nuclear power plants have a long record of safety, vastly more so than those driven by oil or coal, whose fueling and operation across decades have caused countless fatal accidents by fire, by explosion of combustible petroleum products, and by air pollution.

Professor Beckmann did not argue that nuclear power was safe; he correctly pointed out that no form of large-scale energy conversion is safe. Rather, *he argued that nuclear power is far safer than any other form of large-scale energy conversion.* The main reason is the two fundamental pillars of nuclear safety: the slow progress of a nuclear accident—and the defense in depth of nuclear power plants.

Using as one example, the 1979 accident at TMI, he illustrates both principles: within hours a team of experts was flown in and engaged in "what if" horror scenarios. What if the pump cooling the core failed? They still had the other primary loop. What if that failed? They still had the Emergency Core Cooling System (ECCS). What if both loops failed because the power failed? They still had a stand-by diesel generator. What if that also failed? They flew in another one—which, of course, was never needed.

Within hours from the accident's beginning...Hours? They had hours? "How long does it take for an oil tanker to blow up?...What 843 MW facility, other than nuclear, gives you that kind of time to take countermeasures?..." How do you evacuate the population when a dam breaks? How do you take preventive measures while a gasoline refinery blows up?

> Since this book was published [1976], dam disasters have killed thousands of people (at least 2,000 in India in August 1979); many hundreds have died in explosions and fires of gas, oil, butane, gasoline, and other fuels; and tens of thousands have died premature deaths, in the U.S. alone, due to the use of coal. Many of these deaths could have been avoided by using nuclear power as a preferred source of electricity...

Beckmann's thesis was brilliantly illustrated in the accidents incurred at the Japanese nuclear facilities at Fukushima in March 2011. Some of the plants' protective systems remained operational *despite absorbing the twin blows of a colossal (9.0 on the Richter scale) earthquake and an even more colossal thirty-foot tsunami.* Days and even a week later, the U.S. media was hyping the possibility of a large-scale nuclear disaster. (Days and a week later? See above.) In the event, the danger was limited to the release of radiation. At its height, a human being would have had to stand directly outside the plant for four to six hours to absorb an amount of radiation (2,400 microsieverts) that the average person receives annually from natural sources. But since the back-up emergency systems functioned effectively, the area was evacuated of civilians and few persons absorbed levels of radiation that high. The human death toll, if there is any, will be very low—much lower than if fossil-driven plants or hydro-electric dams of an equivalent size were similarly battered by natural forces.

The trend from non-industrial to industrial civilization is toward greatly diminished environmental pollution, a trend emphatically continued by nuclear power. Nevertheless, as one green organization revealingly stated: "We don't want safe nuclear power. We want no nuclear power." Translation: Our stated concern for safety and pollution is a mere smoke screen. What we really oppose is: human-life-enhancing technology.

In retarding development of nuclear power, environmentalists have contributed to the amount of—and danger from—water and atmospheric pollution.

For example, apprehension of this point, and related ones, is central to understanding the causes of British Petroleum's massive 2010 oil spill. Environmentalist restrictions were directly responsible both for the mess and for retarding men's ability to clean it. First, as already stated, by opposing nuclear power, environmentalists have necessarily made America more dependent on oil, consequently more susceptible to serious accidents involving oil. Second, environmentalist restrictions have prohibited drilling in shallow waters proximate to the coast, where divers can operate, making possible quick, effective capping of gushing wells. Instead, they have pushed oil companies far offshore into waters miles deep, where divers cannot function, and where the enormous water pressure changes chemical reactions that occur normally at sea level; making it a monumental technological challenge to cap geysering wells. Third, if it remains necessary to drill for oil in such waters, then applied scientists will, in time, develop technologies capable of effectively capping deep water spills; just as they developed technology to drill for petroleum, to cap shallow water oil spills, to construct jet planes, to build transcontinental railroads, to create international communication via cell phones and the Internet, to construct nuclear power plants and nuclear submarines able to journey beneath the polar ice cap, to fly in space, to journey to the moon, to land probes on Mars, etc.; and they will accomplish this despite, not because of, an environmentalist movement that chronically opposes technological and industrial advance.

Further, it may or may not have been feasible to simply burn the oil, thereby transforming a serious water pollution problem into a minor air pollution one; but regardless the practicality of such a proposal, environmentalists would never have considered, much less supported it. One major reason they would not endorse such a policy? The ensuing air pollution would so quickly dissipate in the atmosphere's vast reaches that it would obviate all occasion to "catastrophize," i.e., to wail regarding a severe man-made calamity and call shrilly for draconian legislation to prevent further incidents.

In fact, regardless of environmentalist propaganda, how "severe" was the "calamity?"

In the event, as reported in a peer-reviewed article in the highly respected journal, *Science*, most of the methane and oil released by the massive spill were devoured by naturally occurring microbes in the Gulf of Mexico. A report in the January 7, 2011 edition of *The Wall Street Journal*, cited the *Science* study, and stated: "Bacteria made quick work of the tons of methane that billowed into the Gulf...The federally funded field study, published online in the journal *Science*, offers peer-reviewed evidence that naturally occurring microbes in the Gulf devoured significant amounts of toxic chemicals in oil and natural gas spewing from the seafloor..." According to federal officials managing the cleanup, "...there was no longer any significant oil from the spill left offshore..."

Man-made accidents do not and cannot approximate the destructive impact of real calamities caused by such nonhuman natural phenomena as earthquakes, tsunamis, volcanoes, lethal epidemics, etc.

Advances in science, technology, and industrialization—not the noxious propaganda of the greens—cleanse man's environment. The man-made environmental messes faced by men in technologically advanced societies possess but a fraction of the virulence of the man-made ones in technologically backward ones. A critical point regarding industrialization is that the human life expectancy did not reach thirty-five years in the mid-eighteenth century, the years immediately preceding Great Britain's Industrial Revolution; subsequently climbed to the mid-to-late seventies; and continue—in the industrialized world—despite plant emissions and oil spills—to rise.

It should be recognized that the *overwhelming preponderance of environmental pollution is caused by nonhuman natural forces*. In 1978, the EPA suppressed a scientific studying showing that up to 80 percent of air pollution was caused by natural, not man-made phenomena. It took a lawsuit, filed under the Freedom of Information Act, to pry the report out of them. One leading source of air pollution widely ignored by the greens is volcanoes. According to Dr. William Pecora, former director of the United States Geological Survey, just three of the myriad eruptions in the past 130 years (Krakatoa, Indonesia, 1883; Katmai, Alaska, 1912; and Hekla, Iceland, 1947) produced more particulate and gaseous pollution of the atmosphere than *the combined activities of all the human beings who ever lived.* This brief list includes neither the other volcanoes of the past 130 years nor the innumerable ones occurring in the earth's vast geologic history prior to those years.

Just one of these was the spectacular eruption of Tambora on the island of Sumbawa in Indonesia in 1815. According to Bill Bryson, in his excellent book, *A Short History of Nearly Everything*, it was the most immense volcanic eruption in ten thousand years, one hundred fifty times the size of the 1980 Mount St. Helens blast, generating a force equivalent to sixty thousand Hiroshima-sized atomic bombs. *"Thirty-six cubic miles of smoky ash, dust, and grit...*diffused through the atmosphere, obscuring the sun's rays and causing the earth to cool." (Emphasis added.) As the colossal volcanic cloud made its way throughout the atmosphere, "the world existed under an oppressive, dusky pall." The year, 1816, became known as "the year without a summer," because temperatures dropped, frosts continued into June and even July, growing seasons shortened, crops failed, and thousands of human beings in the northern hemisphere perished of famine.

Further, over geologic time, many millions of years before man, occurred several widespread mass extinctions that wiped out most life on earth; the most catastrophic, at the end of the Permian period some 250 million years ago, extirpated roughly 95 percent of the planet's life forms. According to such geologists as Anthony Hallam and paleobiologists as Douglas Erwin, massive volcanoes most likely caused the end-Triassic mass extinction some 199 million years in the past; and possibly that of the end-Permian one, as well. One causal factor, though not the only, is the immense volume of sulfur disgorged into the stratosphere, then carried far beyond the blast zone, and resulting in prolonged periods of acid rain.

(The end-Cretaceous mass extinction that obliterated the dinosaurs roughly sixty-five million years ago was almost certainly caused by a massive extra terrestrial object, possibly an asteroid, smashing into the present-day Mexican Yucatan Peninsula.

The destructive power of Mother Nature is awe-inspiring to behold. This tragic truth was demonstrated once again by the massive Japanese earthquake and tsunami of March 2011. By the end of that month, eight thousand human beings were confirmed dead, twelve thousand were missing (most of them presumably crushed and swept out to sea), and immense property damage incurred.)

In April 2010, an eruption of the Eyjafjallajokull volcano on Iceland wreaked havoc in the skies over Europe. The liberal media reported on the thousands of air flights canceled, and the frustrated travelers stranded for days in foreign airports—but said little about the immense amount of air pollution generated, an amount dwarfing—by many orders of magnitude—that produced were it possible to burn off the BP oil spill.

In addition to volcanoes, there are numerous other examples. Swamps are by far the worst source of methane pollution—and *Public Works*, the official publication of Oregon's EPA, divulged that methane from "burping" cows is the leading source of greenhouse gas (GHG) pollution in America, responsible for annually disgorging some fifty million tons of methane into the atmosphere. It must be made clear that Mother Nature, not man's automobiles or factories, is by far the greatest source of GHG pollution.

Advances in applied science and industry cleanse the environment—the *human environment*—and represent an enormous, unparalleled boon to man's earthly life.

Observe the green's equivocation on the term "environment." Logically, the term is a relational concept, referring to the surroundings of some being(s). Why do the greens relentlessly employ this term, rather than the nonrelational concept "nature?" Because it enables them to seduce the uncritical into believing they care about *man's surroundings* and do so because they care about human life. But once having lured in the unwary, the environmentalists proceed to alter the term's meaning to one that denotes "nature" independent of any value to human beings, and often in lethal conflict with man's interest. Peter Schwartz makes this point brilliantly in his essay, "The Philosophy of Privation" in Rand's *Return of the Primitive*:

> ...he [the environmentalist] initially counts on its correct meaning, so that people accept a need to care about the fate of the 'environment'—which they assume in some way is *their* environment and is linked to *their* fate...But once a confused public has been taken in, environmentalists repackage "environment" to denote something upheld as existing separately from human beings.

To be blunt: environmentalists consistently and relentlessly uphold the interest of nonhuman nature—yew trees, owls, swamps euphemistically referred to as "wetlands," jungles euphemistically referred to as "rain forests," laboratory mice, and even germs!—for example, according to green activist, David Ehrenfeld, the final existing supply of smallpox virus must not be extirpated, for it victimizes "solely" human beings. They uphold such "values" in implacable opposition to human health, prosperity, and lives.

Why?

The answer lies in their full philosophy—their metaphysics, ethics, and politics.

A first part of that answer resides in the environmentalist claim of nature's "intrinsic value"—a worth it purportedly possesses independent of any utilitarian value it may hold for man. For example, they value wilderness not because it provides human beings timber or shade or beautiful vistas or backpacking adventure; not because it is home to species that, in some form, advance human purpose or well-being; but solely as an end in itself. A nonhuman natural phenomenon is esteemed by them purely as a distinct, autonomous existent, a regard in no way tarnished if fully inimical to human life.

One environmentalist writer, David Graeber, for example, stated that he is one who "value[s] wilderness for its own sake, not for what value it confers upon mankind... We are not interested in the utility of a particular species, or free-flowing river, or eco-system to mankind. They have intrinsic value, more value—to me—than another human body or a billion of them. Human happiness...[is] not as important as a wild and healthy planet...Until such time as homo sapiens should decide to rejoin nature, some of us can only *hope for the right virus to come along*." (Emphasis added.)

The hope for a deadly virus to efface significant numbers of human lives might still be held solely by the movement's lunatic fringe, although becoming increasing vocalized in mainstream culture. (Graeber's claim was published in *The Los Angeles Times*.) But it is simply the logically consistent conclusion of the movement's basic premise; for if trees, prairies, and field mice, etc., are of significant worth in and of themselves, then man's exploitation of them to build homes or grow crops or cure disease represents a flagrant trespass, a violation of that which innately possesses superlative grandeur and moral standing—and such heinous transgressions surely merit retribution. As such, Graeber's expressed hope for mankind's apocalyptic day of reckoning either already is, or will shortly be, of the movement's essence.

43

The claim that nature has "intrinsic value," that it is worthy of our esteem, even veneration, quite apart from any utilitarian purpose it might serve, is the key to understanding environmentalism. Man, on this view, is an intruder, an eco-nuisance—even scourge—who despoils the sacred natural environment he inhabits. Observe the numerous attempts to transform environmentalism into a quasi-religion. Former New Left leader, Tom Hayden, taught a course at Santa Monica College entitled "Environment and Spirituality," in which he stressed that "we need to see nature as having a sacred quality, so that we revere it and are in awe of it." The Eco-Forestry Institute, in a full-page ad opposing the logging of trees, claimed that trees have intrinsic value and argued that the protection of forests "is more than an economic or ecological issue. It is a spiritual one as well."

Paul Ehrlich, notorious for relentlessly erroneous predictions of catastrophic death tolls from worldwide famine—caused not by political dictatorships eradicating private property and thereby stifling economic development—but by human population growth outstripping the earth's physical capacity to grow sufficient food—predictably bases his claims in faith, rather than in reason and science. "It is probably in vain that so many look to science and technology to solve our present ecological crisis," he wrote. "Much more basic changes are needed, perhaps of the type exemplified by the...hippie movement—a movement that adopts most of its religious ideas from the non-Christian East. It is a movement wrapped up in Zen Buddhism, physical love and a disdain for physical wealth."

Additionally, Carl Sagan issued a call for a religious crusade on behalf of environmentalist values. "We are close to committing—many would say we are already committing—what in religious language is sometimes called Crimes against Creation," he said. Environmentalism "must be recognized as having a religious as well as a scientific dimension."

What makes rats holy? In what sense are mosquitoes sacred? Why are malarial swamps venerated—but human life is not? The environmentalists offer no rational answers to such questions—do not even attempt an answer—because there are none.

From a religious metaphysics, of any kind, logically follows a self-sacrifice ethic. Human beings are enjoined to render unquestioning obedience and/or provide selfless service to the deity. The sacred is held as apart from and above human life—and man is consequently denigrated relative to a hallowed ruling power. It is this purported sacredness of nature—its inherent value—its venerable status independent of and, often, in opposition to the requirements of man's life—that leads, logically and inexorably, to incessant calls to sacrifice the human to the nonhuman. Why cannot we perform medical research on rodents? Why is it wrong to exploit trees in an attempt to cure cancer? Why is it unethical to drill for oil in miserably frozen northern tundra? These and similar moral questions are answered in a manner logically consistent with environmentalism's religious fundamentals: Because the nonhuman is holy—and the human is not. The profane—man—must be sacrificed to the sacred—nature.

Any form of religion ineluctably denigrates man. Whether of a form transcendent, as Christianity—or immanent, as environmentalism—it seeks reverence in that which dwarfs human ability. God is an awesome fantasy; nature an awesome reality; but shared in common is their respective worshippers' hungry quest to identify an all-powerful force before which to prostrate themselves. Observe the unremitting cynicism of religion—its extreme pessimism regarding human virtue and value—an insatiable appetite to diminish man relative to some overwhelming being ever ready to retribute his "transgressions." Religion's loathing of man is so uniformly consistent it repeatedly demands punishment for his virtues and achievements; prime examples are banishment from "paradise" for the "sin" of gaining moral knowledge—and calls for a lethally pandemic virus for such "crimes against creation" as expunging mosquitoes and performing medical experiments on rats.

Self-loathing, in a generic, no less than an individual form, is a tragically enduring attitude—rampant during the Dark and Middle Ages—masquerading, in the twenty-first century, as a trendy, avant-garde "idealism." Millions of human beings seek the worshipful in something of power vastly superior to the human, before which man is to humbly abase himself.

Environmentalism—as any other religion—venerates the nonhuman precisely because it is nonhuman.

Regarding nature as of solely utilitarian value is—to environmentalists—akin to telling Christians that their God should be so evaluated. Such a claim is blasphemous. It inverts the proper order of value. It subordinates the rightfully reverential to the debased; the consecrated to the desecrated. It is not properly the god who serves man—but man who serves god. Sacrifice of the lowly being before the all-powerful, all-good one is mandated.

Regarding politics, environmentalists are necessarily statists—unreconstituted collectivists and socialists, who hold that an individual's life belongs not to him but to the state. Is there a single supporter of egoism, individual rights, and laissez-faire capitalism among them? If so, the author is unaware of him. He is either nonexistent or, at best, possesses a voice both pianissimo and drowned by the movement's monolithic and cacophonous yowling for statism.

Socialists, dismayed by the collapse of Communism in the Soviet Union and its East European empire, co-opted environmentalism. The economist, Walter Williams, accurately refers to environmentalists as "watermelons"—green on the outside, red on the inside. For if they can convince sufficient voters that economic growth under capitalism entails baleful environmental degradation, they can thereby gain political/legal control over the "offending" businesses and industries. Environmentalism, in short, represents a viable backdoor into socialism.

Logically, a self-sacrifice ethic in any iteration entails a statist, anti-individualist politics. If a man is morally obligated to render selfless service to a being greater than he—whether God, society, or nature—one urgent question is: how to effectively impose such noble edicts on those too recalcitrantly selfish to voluntarily comply? The answer is manifest: legally empower the government to coercively enforce an individual's duty to the higher power.

If Christianity (or Judaism or Islam) is culturally dominant in a society, then theocracy is the inescapable political result; for moral virtue requires undeviating obeisance to God's commandments; man's law must be compliant with God's law; and the sole way to ensure it is for the state to be governed by those who best know God's will—the clergy and theologians—who deploy its police power to legally enforce God's laws.

Similarly, if a Marxist (or National Socialist) creed is culturally dominant: an individual then owes unstinting service to the working class (or race). Again, the sole method of ensuring commission of such duties is to grant totalitarian power to the state to police them.

The logic here is endlessly replicable. If nonhuman nature is sacred, and to be preserved in pristine character, then it is mandatory that the "environmental police" be granted sufficient power to punish any and all transgressions against its inviolable rights. The establishment of an environmentalist police state is logically inevitable. The EPA began just such a police state on January 2, 2011 to punish emitters of "greenhouse gases," in accordance with their parable of "man-made global warming."

What becomes of human life if the environmentalist philosophy becomes culturally dominant and its consequent political authoritarianism enacted? Graeber offers a clue—one repeated by many of his peers. He stated: "Until such time as homo sapiens decide to *rejoin nature...*" (Emphasis added.) The premise here articulated is that *technological and industrial society is outside the parameters of nature—and in sharp conflict with it.*

What would it look like for man to "rejoin" nature? For if nonhuman nature has innate value, it follows that man must not disturb it even to fell trees for log cabins, clear land for crops, or fill in bogs to eradicate disease-bearing mosquitoes. On the logic of environmentalist premises, man is to *revert back not merely to a pre-industrial—but to a pre-agricultural stage.* He is to live like American Indians—or like pre-historic man—as hunters/gatherers.

With no medicine to cure disease, at the mercy of storm, blight, and pestilence, having no recourse but starvation when vegetative and animal life are killed by drought, the human life expectancy reverts to twenty-odd years and living standards to those so abysmally low that, by contrast, the penury of contemporary Third World nations seems lush opulence.

The superb American economist, Julian Simon, edited a book, *The State of Humanity*, that provides a plethora of factual data supporting such claims. For example: "Most of these records suggest that life expectancy from prehistoric times until 1400 or so was in the range of 20–30 years." Further, there existed "a probability of death by age five among primitive hunter-gatherer peoples of between 400 and 500 per thousand." If forty to fifty percent of the human population perished by age five, it is heartbreaking but not surprising that average expectancy of life did not exceed, and perhaps did not reach, thirty years.

Man is, indeed, part of nature; he is an evolutionary development of nature, as are all of earth's life forms; and, like them, must seek survival in accordance with *his nature.* By grace of nature's laws, man evolved as a rational being. His intelligence is not an accident—but his naturally developed means of survival. He cannot fly like a bird or run like a cheetah or employ claws and fangs with which to rend prey; he does not burrow warrens beneath the earth or grow thicker fur in winter or migrate with the seasons. Such characteristics and activities are not of *his nature.* Nature endows man with a certain type of brain—one enabling him to make advances in agricultural science and technology, and thereby to grow food; to build homes and cities; to cure disease; to live in accordance with human nature.

Man is an *intelligent* being—by entire orders of magnitude the most intelligent creation of nature's majestic evolutionary process—a being who survives and flourishes solely because of application of such intelligence to problems of practical living.

Man's nature is part of, has evolved from and in congruence with that of nonhuman nature. There is no inherent conflict between nonhuman nature and human beings prospering in accordance with the kind of being they are. Such a hypothetical clash would entail a dichotomy between human survival requirements and the laws of nature *within and in accordance with which they arose.* Such a logical impossibility is no more than a contrived environmentalist delusion. Nature requires living organisms to take active, often constructive, steps to enhance their lives. As beavers construct dams, birds build nests, gophers burrow holes, etc., in accordance with the necessities nature mandates for their survival—so man clears forests, grows crops, erects cities, constructs mines, etc., in accordance with nature's requirements of his. *Man is never so much a part of nature as when, by means of rational intelligence, he deploys the natural resources of his environment as a means of achieving life-giving utilitarian purposes.*

This leads to the fatal flaw of environmentalist philosophy. To hold that X—nature or anything else—has value, pre-supposes an answer to the question: value to whom? There is no such thing as "value" in the absence of a valuer. Graeber acknowledges as much when he writes: "They [free-flowing rivers, wilderness, etc.] have intrinsic value, more value—*to me*—than another human body, or a billion of them." (Emphasis added.) Sadly for Graeber, billions of human beings value the high living standards and increased life expectancies that accrue from agricultural science, medical research, technological development, and industrialization. Should their values be sacrificed to his? If so, why? Why should millions of human beings perish from a lethal virus to satisfy his desire for untrammeled wilderness? Why should billions of humans subsist in abysmal penury so that mice, mosquitoes, and swamps might flourish? Why should nature's highest evolutionary creation—highest in terms of biological sophistication, brain power, and intellectual achievement—be subordinated to those vastly lower? There is no rational answer to such questions—only the faith-based assertions discussed above.

Values exist solely because organisms must gain specific ends to attain flourishing life. *Fully self-actualized, prospering life, in accordance with an organism's distinctive nature, is always and necessarily the goal.* Healthy, fulfilled life is the single goal in existence that is an end in itself; all other goals are subordinate means to that greater end. It is to attain such an ultimate goal—and only for such purpose—that the phenomenon of valuing comes into existence.

To a substantial degree, nonhuman species find their values ready-made in nature—be it vegetative life to eat, herbivores to devour, rain water, sunlight, or fertile soil, etc. Nonhuman species survive by killing each other—they eat plants or other animals, virulent microbes kill host organisms, etc.—but their survival necessitates no need to dramatically transform their habitat. The years and activities of their full life span leave their surroundings virtually untouched. A pride of lions or a herd of antelopes might continue for millennia or longer with no significant alteration to the plains they inhabit. Their nature provides them neither means nor need to adapt their environment to themselves. What would a lion, for example, do with a townhouse, automobile, interstate highways, river-spanning bridges, cities, and a ticket to a Broadway show? Such species adapt to their surroundings, and if such proves impossible they perish.

But flourishing human life entails the achievement of contrasting values.

For example: can any one specify the outermost limits of the human life expectancy? Prior to the Industrial Revolution it stood in the mid-thirties. Today, in the industrialized nations, for an infant girl it is roughly eighty. Some researchers believe that by means of genetic engineering, stem cell research, and cloning of vital organs, it could reach triple digits—and do so this century. Perhaps, it can be extended even farther than that.

But none of this is possible in the absence of vast quantities of antecedent agricultural, technological, and industrial advance. For man to flourish—to prosper, to self-actualize, to live to the fullest as the kind of being nature created—he must plant extensive acreage of crops, domesticate and eat livestock, erect homes and cities, etc. He can and must transfigure his natural surroundings in accordance with his life requirements. *His nature is not that of any other species—and nature does not permit him to prosper via the methods suitable to them.*

Nonhuman nature, to environmentalists, is generally benign; man, by contrast, an arrantly wanton despoiler. Their malevolent hostility to the latter stands in direct proportion to their sappy drooling over the former. Both claims are flagrantly false. Regarding the furtherance of human life, man, though a destroyer when choosing unreason, can and often does choose reason, creating thereby philosophy, science, the arts, agriculture, commerce, cities, and flourishing civilization. Nonhuman nature, although supporting life via brilliant sunshine, resuscitating rain, and fecund soil, quite as often extinguishes it by means of volcano, earthquake, tsunami, virulent plague, and comet/asteroid impact. Although earth is our home, and we its guests, it is often a host quite inhospitable; by giving rise to man's rational nature, it makes his life possible; but natural phenomena more baleful renders it immensely daunting and often sadly abridged. The forces of nonhuman—one is tempted to say "inhuman"—nature are colossally more powerful for destruction than the relatively puny forces of man.

The good, for man, is that which factually, objectively—given the kind of being he is—supports his life. Does this include clean air and water, and a planet filled with vibrantly alive vegetative and animal species? Unequivocally—yes.

But the criterion of moral value is that which promotes human life—nonhuman nature as it serves man's utilitarian requirements, not nonhuman nature as an ends in itself. The first is a good to be joyously celebrated; the second, an evil to be implacably opposed.

Natural Resources

The greatest natural resource, by far, is not oil, iron ore, coal, fertile agricultural lands, or anything of the kind. It is the human mind. The outstanding American economist, Julian Simon, makes this vital point in his excellent book, *The Ultimate Resource.* In *Atlas Shrugged,* Ayn Rand makes it even more forcefully.

Make no mistake about this: the rational mind is a creation of nature—it is nature's most exalted creation—and it constitutes, by many orders of magnitude, the natural resource most vital for human survival and prosperity.

The critical principle regarding this issue is: given the unfettered freedom of the rational mind in a system of laissez-faire capitalism, *it is impossible—not unlikely, but impossible—to run out of natural resources.*

How can this be?—honest men might ask. Afterall, they point out, oil, coal, iron, etc., are finite, not inexhaustible; at some point, surely, they will be depleted. This is an honest but mistaken objection, and, in refutation, several points must be made.

A relatively minor point is that, according to estimates of the United States Geological Survey, amounts of natural resources existing in the earth's crust, even at increased rates of consumption, are sufficient to last for thousands of years.

A more important point is an economic one. When any resource begins to grow scarce, its price rises. This motivates entrepreneurial individuals to seek either a new and plentiful supply of the valued resource—or one capable of substituting for it. Examine the historical evidence. In medieval Europe, for example, the main source of energy was charcoal from wood. When wood began to grow scarce, people sought other means of fuel. They eventually found it in chunks of black rock previously thought useless—coal.

Centuries later, in the mid-1800s, some people feared that man was running out of coal. When its price rose, innovators were encouraged to seek other energy sources. For years, farmers in western Pennsylvania had been plagued by the presence of a viscous black liquid that damaged their crops and tainted their pastures. Nobody saw any practical value in it. Finally, some entrepreneurs conceived its possibilities, and, in 1859, founded the Pennsylvania Rock Oil Company of Titusville, Pennsylvania. Shortly thereafter, the firm was successful in digging for oil. Further, when men began to fear the depletion of Earth's petroleum supplies, one solution became the use of uranium to generate vast amounts of nuclear power. Today, America can and should follow France's lead in development of this virtually inexhaustible energy supply.

The explanatory principle is that of: substitutability. Human beings do not care about coal or oil or uranium, etc. They want safe, inexpensive energy to power their electric appliances and automobiles (among other things). The specific natural resource that provides such power is not their concern. There is no resource so inimitable that its effect cannot be satisfactorily replicated from alternative sources—and probably myriad of them. In the twenty-first century, for example, men employ fiber optic cables, in place of copper, in wire phone lines. Such glass fibers are derived from quartz sand. *Sand.*

In virtually every instance, various means are capable of supplying the same result. Oil or natural gas can heat homes as effectively as can coal. Buses or commuter trains may get employees to work as efficiently as automobiles. Such synthetic fabrics as rayon or nylon can be substituted for cotton in the manufacture of clothing. Chicken or tuna might provide a man as much protein as beef. Nuclear power can replace fossil fuels as the means of generating electricity. Cellular technology might replace conventional land lines as the basic means of telephone communication. The principle of infinite substitutability stipulates that the service provided by one substance can be effectively duplicated by others.

According to evolutionary biology, man—*homo sapiens*—has inhabited the earth for roughly two hundred thousand years. During that entire span, vast petroleum deposits lay beneath his feet, potentially useable as a source of energy. But it was considered utterly useless, even baneful, because the human mind had not yet identified any utilitarian purpose for it. Similarly, aluminum, the most abundant metal in the earth's crust, became productively useable only within the past century, as men's knowledge of metallurgy increased. The same is true of uranium, of sand, and, in some form throughout history, of every other substance on earth.

The earth is a solidly packed ball of matter, roughly four thousand miles to the core from any point on its surface; men have dug, at most, ten miles deep—barely, literally scratching its surface. *Every inch, every millimeter, every cubic foot of the earth's matter is a resource.* Every ounce of such resources is potentially beneficial to human life. All that is necessary is that the free-thinking human mind identify a resource's specific use and the manner to best exploit it.

Listen for a moment to a spokesman for the doomsayers: "You must know that the world has grown old, and does not remain in its former vigor. It bears witness to its own decline. The rainfall and the sun's warmth are both diminishing; the metals are nearly exhausted; the [farmer] is failing in the fields…" *The metals are nearly exhausted.* These melancholy lines were composed in the third century AD, in the days of the Roman Empire, before men conceived any use for aluminum, uranium, coal, oil, or iron's role in manufacturing steel. Today, with vastly less excuse, environmentalists express the same lachrymose sentiments.

The primary point always overlooked by the environmentalist doomsayers, of course, is the inexhaustible ingenuity of man's mind. If sand can be effectively deployed in fiber optic technology, then what uses can the mind discover for various other common substances?

What uses for sea water, for example? What for shale rock? What for sunlight, wind, even organic waste? The truth is that human intelligence has already identified numerous future employments for such resources, some in the near term.

Ocean water, for example, contains vast amounts of natural resources. Technology expert, Herman Kahn, wrote: "Calculations indicate that every cubic kilometer of seawater contains approximately 37.5 million tons of solids in solution or suspension. The major portion of this consists of sodium and chlorine, but there is also an enormous amount of magnesium, and varying but relatively large quantities of gold, cobalt, lead, mercury, and many other minerals." Related, available methods already make it possible to obtain specific substances from the sea. For example, both Germany and Japan have initiated projects to extract uranium directly from seawater.

Further, there exist enormous quantities of natural resources—among them oil, nickel, copper, manganese, and cobalt—that can be derived by mining the ocean floor; mining for which, in some cases, the technology already exists.

Shale rock—and tar sands, as well—contain vast amounts of potential fuel. According to estimates of the highly respected Hudson Institute, the fuel available from shale and tar sands, combined with the other fossil sources of oil, natural gas, and coal, could provide the earth's entire population with sufficient fuel for centuries, even factoring into the equation a future increased demand for energy. The technology exists to accomplish this today—but, currently, other means of energy production are less expensive. If, in the future, oil, natural gas, and coal become scarcer, consequently more expensive, and/or innovative methods of extracting fuel from shale and tar sands reduce the process' cost, these sources will be developed.

Ocean thermal power, in which electrical energy is derived from the sun-warmed surface waters of the ocean, offers a limitless source of electricity. Geothermal energy—the enormous heat contained within the earth—is another potential source of power. Some scientists estimate that a geothermal resource base exists in the United States sufficient to provide the world's energy needs for centuries. Even bio-conversion—a process of obtaining energy by converting organic materials, especially wastes, to fuel—is feasible. This process is especially intriguing because it could take all organic waste from cities, agriculture, and industry, and convert it into usable energy.

53

Some scoff that such hopes are arrant science fiction. These are the same mentalities who, centuries earlier, could conceive of no possible uses for either coal or oil; who snickered at the presumption that men might fly; who could not dream of telephone technology, nuclear power, or space travel; and who would have regarded as sheerest lunacy the notion that sand might be deployed to construct fiber optic cables. Such individuals sadly limit the application of their own minds, and so, inevitably, find inconceivable the creative, expansive capacities of others.

Further, the earth's moon—and the solar system's other planets—are uninhabited. They, too, like the earth, are solidly packed balls of matter, every ounce of which is a potentially usable natural resource. Many science fiction stories—notably Robert Heinlein's classic *The Moon is a Harsh Mistress*—depict such barren worlds transformed into mining colonies by productive men. In the future, as with submarines, airplanes, and space travel, such science fiction will become science-based reality. As one supporter of human life, mocking environmentalism, stated aptly: "Earth First. Then mine the other planets."

There *is* a sense in which natural resources are finite—but it is only in the metaphysical sense that all things are finite, including human needs, desires, and life expectancies. *To be is to be finite.* Whatever exists—regardless its vast immensity—including entire galaxies or interlocking combinations of such—is delimited to a specific identity, including in terms of quantity. It is what it is—that is all that it is—and there is no more. Any existent—and all in total—are finite.

Environmentalists sometimes make the erroneous claim that resources are finite—but human desires infinite—implying a logical clash between the two. There is no such conflict, because the premise is egregiously false. A secondary but still significant truth is that under the freedom and wealth of the capitalist system, birth rates decline; in time, a free country's population increase by natural reproduction (rather than by immigration) ceases. One reason for this is that women, with their inalienable individual rights protected by law, possess myriad opportunities to find fulfillment in education, career, etc., not solely in marriage and motherhood. A stable (or possibly declining) population places natural limits on demand.

But a vastly more important point is a philosophical one. No matter an explosive growth of human population, or the immense extent of human needs, wants, or desires—any conceivable number or amount represents a finite figure. An individual, or a group of them, might desire ten trillion dollars of wealth—or a billion trillion dollars—or any amount imaginable—nevertheless, the resulting sum, however colossal, is unalterably, irrevocably finite. As Aristotle established long ago, the infinite exists solely as a potential. Any existing reality, including human demand, is finite. There is no logical difficulty entailed by a finite being exploiting finite resources in service of finite needs.

Finally, bear in mind that the sun's life expectancy, as any star's, is also finite. Some day, in roughly ten billion years, it will expire—and bring to an end all life in a then sunless little corner of the Milky Way Galaxy. Will human life end then? Or will man migrate to the stars? On the extremely pessimistic view of the environmentalists, given their narrow, self-limiting conception of the mind's potential, the sun's demise will signal mankind's doom. But on a more realistic view, human advances in rational philosophy and science—giving rise to an expansive, brimming, "can-do" optimism—will make possible human colonization of uninhabited planets in distant star systems. Man's body—and his spirit—will live on.

Global Warming or Climate Change

The dominant theory underlying and giving rise to proposed cap and trade legislation (and to the similar, earlier Kyoto Protocol) is that of man-made or anthropogenic global warming (AGW). This is the claim that human industrialization spews into the atmosphere untold quantities of carbon dioxide (CO_2) thereby intensifying the earth's greenhouse effect, leading to catastrophic warming. To fully, definitively defeat attempts to reduce GHG emissions by means of coercive governmental legislation, its underlying theory must be disproven.

Climate change, whether warming or cooling, is driven by enormously complex natural factors, only some of which are understood in our day. The claim that GHGs are the predominant driving force of climate change is fatuous, and, more important, demonstrably false. The claim that human economic development is the main progenitor of CO_2 is equally erroneous.

It is time to cut through the hysteria surrounding this issue—and analyze it rationally. When this is done, it becomes apparent that Al Gore and the environmentalists, the "scientists" at the UN Intergovernmental Panel on Climate Change (IPCC), and their shills in the liberal media are utterly, hopelessly, irrevocably mistaken.

There are three distinct components to the claim of global warming: (1) The earth warmed slightly—roughly one degree

Fahrenheit—during the late-nineteenth and twentieth centuries. (2) This warming was caused by human industrialization and economic development, specifically by discharge into the atmosphere of large quantities of CO_2 and other GHGs. (3) Such warming is pernicious, resulting eventually in dire consequences to life on earth, including human life.

Point One is true. But of immensely greater importance than the small amount of warming that occurred is that: Point Two is irremediably false, as is Point Three.

The scientific data does not support the claim of *man-made* global warming—nor does it validate the charge that a warming trend is catastrophic or even remotely harmful. Rather, the scientific evidence strongly supports the claims that warming is natural, not man-made; and that it is beneficial, not baneful to earthly life. *Charges of man-made global warming are driven fully by considerations philosophical, moral, and political—not by any scientific.*

The first step in establishing this is to present relevant, important facts. The second, critically, is to rationally analyze them.

The Scientific Data

Fact One: Relatively recent history (the past several thousand years) shows the earth cycling repeatedly between warmer and cooler periods. For example, prior to the Modern Warm Period (much of the late-nineteenth and twentieth centuries) existed what historians refer to as the Little Ice Age. This period is dated (roughly) from 1300 to 1850. The earth was generally colder than during the late-nineteenth and twentieth centuries. During this period the Northern Hemisphere was rocked by the severe storms and icing associated with colder weather. In northern Europe, massive death by famine was common, especially during the era's severest period around the turn of the eighteenth century.

Prior to the Little Ice Age existed the Medieval Warm Period, roughly 900–1300 AD. During this era, temperatures were as warm (or warmer) than during the Modern Warm Period. In northern Europe, storms, icing, and catastrophic crop failures were less frequent; grapes were grown in northern climes; ice packs in the North Atlantic were less prevalent, and the Norse settled in parts of Greenland, colonies which survived for centuries but were ultimately crushed by frigid conditions of the Little Ice Age. The Norse successfully cultivated crops there during this era. By contrast, today the island is roughly 80% ice-capped, possesses 0% arable land, and grows

0% permanent crops. Would anyone think to name it "Greenland" in current times?

Prior to the Medieval Warm Period was the Dark Age Cold Period, roughly 600–900 AD. Prior to that was the Roman Warm Period, extending roughly from 200 BC to 600 AD. Prior to that existed an unnamed cold period, roughly 600–200 BC, that pre-dated the Roman Warm Period.

Further, in nature there exist cycles within cycles. For example, although the earth has gradually warmed between the mid-nineteenth century and today as it recovers from the Little Ice Age, it nonetheless cooled between (roughly) 1940 and 1975, precipitating fears, in the 1970s, of a catastrophic trend toward "global cooling" and of a looming ice age. Indeed, *Newsweek*, in its issue of April 28, 1975, published its now infamous essay, "The Cooling World," loudly proclaiming such alarmism. The lesson is not to upbraid alarmists—but to understand that shorter climate cycles in the midst of countervailing longer ones make it extremely difficult to forecast long-term trends.

Fact Two: As already noted, human beings, in some form, have existed for some two hundred thousand years. According to geology, the earth itself is roughly 4.5 *billion* years old. *The earth has a vast climate history independent of human existence.* It reveals significant fluctuations in temperature. For example, some eight hundred million years ago, in the so-called Cryogenian Period, the earth underwent the most colossal ice age of its history. It was so cold that glaciers extended even into tropical regions, and may have covered the entire globe, even the equator. Because of the massive icing, the period is colloquially referred to as: "Snowball Earth." Some 540 million years ago, earth transformed from a frozen "snow ball," into a planet warm and humid. This major climate shift enabled the evolutionary process resulting in the earth's current life forms. Roughly 350 million years ago, northern cooling resulted in ice sheets returning to the higher latitudes. Some three hundred million years ago, the planet was largely hot and humid, with swamp and jungle dominating most land areas. There have been dry, hot periods throughout Earth's long history when evaporite or salt deposits formed that were thousands of feet thick.

More recently, about five million years in the past, a cooling trend in the northern hemisphere led to formation of more glaciers and ice sheets—and, roughly two million years ago, began cyclical ice ages, each lasting for approximately ninety thousand to one hundred thousand years, interspersed with interglacial periods roughly ten thousand to twenty thousand years in duration. Temperature shifts were often abrupt and dramatic. For example, according to leading climatologist, Dr. Fred Singer, about 11,500 years ago originated the present interglacial period (the Holocene).

> The planet warmed from ice age to nearly present world temperatures in less than one hundred years. *Half the warming may have occurred in fifteen years.* Ice sheets melted, sea levels rose again, and forests expanded. Trees replaced grass and grass replaced desert. (Emphasis added.)

The Holocene, it might be noted, while warm relative to the ice ages that preceded and will follow it, is not as warm as some of earth's earlier interglacial periods.

Fact Three: Over geological time, the earth's temperature has ranged from fifty-three degrees to seventy degrees Fahrenheit. In our era the planet's temperature is some 58–59 degrees Fahrenheit, nearer the cooler than the warmer end of the spectrum.

Fact Four: At times in earth's history, much higher concentrations of atmospheric CO_2 than today's have been associated with significantly lower temperatures. For example, the esteemed paleontologist, Dr. Robert Carter, a leading scientific critic of the IPCC's claims, points out that throughout the current Phanerozoic Eon there exist multiple periods of discrepancy between CO_2 levels and temperatures, including a period between 444 and 353 million years ago that saw major glaciation combined with atmospheric levels of CO_2 many times higher than today. Climatologist, Fred Singer, makes an identical point: "CO_2 levels were ten times higher than today's during the frigid Ordovician glacial period about 440 million years ago." American-born paleoclimatologist, Dr. Tim Patterson, concurs: "There is no meaningful correlation between CO_2 levels and Earth's temperature over this [geologic] time frame. In fact, when CO_2 levels were over ten times higher than they are now, about 450 million years ago, the planet was in the depths of the absolute coldest period in the last half billion years."

Fact Five: The earth's present temperature is "warm" or "cool" relative to its past depending on which historical date is selected as a point of reference. For example, geologist, Dr. Doug Macdougall, discussing ice ages in his book, *Frozen Earth*, points out that the earth, today, is very much in the midst of an ice age—in the so-called "inter-glacial warm interval" between ice ages. "...in comparison with the average of the past few million years, the present-day interglacial climate is benign. The last time the earth was as warm as it is today was about 120,000 years ago; for most of the time since then it has been much, much colder." On the other hand, taking a longer-term view, Macdougall notes that for the past fifty or sixty million years the earth has gradually cooled—and was generally significantly warmer in its past, as evidenced by the fossil remains of tropical and subtropical plants and animals found north of the Arctic Circle. The earth is warmer today than it has been at select times in its history—but it is cooler than it has been throughout most of its past.

Glaciers at polar regions and high altitudes have been largely absent. Dr. Macdougall points out: "Fortunately for us, the glaciers have withdrawn to high altitudes and latitudes during the present warm period. But, on average, for the past few million years, the Earth has been considerably colder than over most of its four and a half billion years of existence. During much of Earth history, except for short, rare intervals, glaciers such as the one on Kilimanjaro have been absent."

Throughout most of the earth's voluminous history, it has generally been warmer than during our era.

One important conclusion can be reached based even on such minimal rendering of scientific data: the planet has undergone pronounced climate variations—substantially more extreme than experienced during the Modern Warm Period—long before the inception of human industrialization in late-eighteenth-century Britain; indeed, long before man existed. What caused such extreme climate change? One fact is certain: the answer is to be found in nonhuman nature.

Ice ages, for example—their onset, duration, and terminus—embody variations in temperature significantly more extreme than the minimal climate change of the past century-and-a-half. Most of them occurred before human life originated—and all prior to industrialization. Human beings, therefore, are ruled out as part of the causation.

According to the theory widely accepted by scientists today, the trigger for ice ages lies in the complex astronomical relationship between earth and sun—in a combination of such factors. One of these is the "eccentricity" of the earth's orbit; a second lies in the tilt of the earth's axis; a third is the earth's wobble on that axis. It requires a specific alignment of such factors to trigger an ice age, an alignment that obtains on a roughly one hundred thousand year cycle. Further, even this complex of astronomical factors translates to only very small variations in the amount of solar radiation received on parts of earth's surface; so it is not the full causation of earth's ice ages—but a trigger for other natural, now terrestrial forces, e.g., ice-generated reflection of solar energy, shifting winds, changing ocean currents, etc., that combine to drive down temperatures. The complex interaction of natural forces at play is staggering, and helps explain the profound difficulties in understanding climate science.

One of these natural factors has been recently identified by Israeli astrophysicist, Dr. Nir Shaviv. The major ice ages of the earth's long history have occurred every 142 million years. This timing coincides perfectly with the passage of the earth through the spiral arms of the Milky Way Galaxy, which means the planet is increasingly bombarded by intergalactic cosmic rays, which triggers increasing cloud cover, thereby lowering temperatures. The causal connection between cosmic rays, cloud cover, and global temperatures has been recently discovered by Danish astrophysicist, Dr. Henrik Svensmark, as explained later.

When placed in this broader context of knowledge—one that includes recurrent ice ages set amidst a planet generally significantly warmer than today—and all of it occurring before man even existed—what is to be made of the one degree Fahrenheit rise in global temperature of the past 100–150 years?

No truth can be understood independent of the broader context within which it arises. Would a competent historian, for example, analyze the causes of World War II while omitting examination of WWI's aftermath, the terms imposed on Germany by the Versailles Treaty, and the rise of totalitarianism in Russia, Italy, and Germany? If so, his interpretation would display a sad paucity of understanding.

Like such a tunnel-visioned historian, the IPCC purports to understand the Modern Warm Period independent of the earth's stupendous climate history. Its inexplicable neglect of such pertinent data raises troubling questions. For example: Why should a mere one degree rise in temperature cause alarm when it is minimal, even trivial, in relation to immense climate swings of the past? Why should GHG accumulation now be considered the decisive cause of temperature increase when its vastly greater accumulation has, at times, been associated with frigid earthly conditions? Why were astronomical factors—not GHG—responsible for the pronounced climate change of ice ages and their cessation—and why are similar astronomical factors not to be considered today? Have the laws of nature changed—or been rescinded by IPCC decree? How is man identified with certainty as the cause, while nonhuman nature—responsible for sweeping climate changes throughout geologic history—is not even considered? When the modest temperature change of the Modern Warm Period is plugged into the earth's full climate history, these are questions that demand an answer.

The IPCC has committed a flagrant example of what Ayn Rand termed the "fallacy of context dropping"—of ignoring, denying, or evading the facts that give rise to a phenomenon in question. The cognitive integration that the IPCC refuses to perform is of the essence of objectivity, a method requiring men to, first, support a conclusion with a plethora of factual evidence—and, second, to fit the conclusion seamlessly into a broad cognitive frame of reference. Hegel was quite right in his identification that: "The true is the whole." A true conclusion fits without contradiction into a sweeping range of factual data.

The IPCC rejection of the big picture eliminates from consideration the sweeping range of factual data that would expose as vacuous its charges of "unprecedented warming." Such facts, to it, represent a colossally "inconvenient truth." So it simply refuses to acknowledge them, relying instead on its ability to generate fear amongst a public generally ignorant of geology. The myopic outlook projected by the IPCC constitutes an extreme form of cognitive disintegration, and represents a profound flaw in its reasoning.

But it is not the only one.

The alarmists claim that rising levels of man-made CO_2 constitute the primary cause of rising temperature. Such a conclusion is beset by multiple specific errors. One is that the overwhelming preponderance of atmospheric CO_2 (97%) proceeds from natural, not man-made, sources. A second is that, according to geologists, the IPCC grossly overestimates the duration of man-made CO_2 in the atmosphere. (The IPCC claims 50–200 years, while more than three dozen scientific studies confirm the duration of CO_2 in the atmosphere as 5–12 years; then it is absorbed into the oceans.)

But the alarmists' main error is that: *they have reversed the causation.* It is not rising CO_2 levels that drive temperature increase, but, rather, rising temperatures that drive increasing CO_2 levels. Analysis of the now-famed ice cores from the Antarctic's Vostok Glacier reveals that, for at least the past five hundred thousand years, increasing amounts of atmospheric CO_2 lag, by centuries, behind the rise of earth's temperature. Over this time period, there has indeed been a strong correlation between atmospheric CO_2 and temperature—but *rising CO_2 levels are an effect, not a cause, of rising temperatures.*

Dr. Nir Shaviv, for example, wrote: "In all cases where there is a good enough resolution, one finds that the CO_2 lags behind the temperature by typically several hundred to a thousand years. Thus, the basic climate driver that controls the temperature cannot be that of CO_2." Dr. Robert Carter concurs: "The ice-core data show conclusively that, during natural climate cycling, changes in temperature precede changes in carbon dioxide by an average 800 years or so." Czech physicist, Dr. Lubos Motl, a former professor at Harvard, agrees. He wrote on his blog: "The temperatures and carbon dioxide concentrations have been correlated...but we know for sure that the temperature was the cause and the concentration was its consequence, not the other way around." It has long been known by scientists that the ocean's immense capacity to store gases decreases with temperature increase. Therefore, as the earth warms, the oceans are able to store less CO_2—and more of it is released into the atmosphere.

But if rising CO_2 levels are not *the* cause of temperature increase—indeed, in some cases, not even *a* cause—then what is? Not surprisingly, the answer harks back to the trigger of earth's ice ages: the enormous complexity of the sun's processes—and its interactions with other cosmic factors. In addition to what is known regarding the cause of ice ages, there is another fact pointing to the sun as prime cause of the current warming: NASA's recent confirmation of warming on Mars. Eminent Russian physicist, Dr. Habibullo Abdussamatov, dismisses IPCC claims disdainfully: "Mars has global warming," he says, "but without a greenhouse and without the participation of Martians."

The sun cycles: at times it emits less radiation, at times more. Abdussamatov confirms conclusions reached from analysis of Vostok ice cores: "It is no secret that increased solar irradiance warms Earth's oceans, which then triggers the emission of large amounts of carbon dioxide into the atmosphere. So the common view that man's industrial activities is a deciding factor in global warming has emerged from a misinterpretation of cause-and-effect relations."

Although the disparity in solar irradiation is, in itself, relatively small, its earthly effect is amplified by other factors. Danish scientist, Dr. Henrik Svensmark, and other astrophysicists, have made major breakthroughs in recent years in explaining the sun–climate connection. Here, in plain terms, is the state-of-the-art research that Al Gore and IPCC scientists simply ignore.

Meteorologists have long known that low-lying cloud cover helps keeps the earth cool. (The intelligent layman, having experienced many cloudy days, knows it too.) In his book, *The Chilling Stars*, Dr. Svensmark writes: "Strange to say, the experts on weather and climate never really knew where the clouds came from." Now they do. The ascending theory in astrophysics is that cosmic rays (energy released by exploding stars, i.e., super novae) enter earth's atmosphere and release electrons in the air; these then encourage "the clumping of molecules to make micro-specks, capable of gathering into the larger specks needed for cloud formation."

In 2006, Svensmark and his team established this experimentally. They allowed naturally occurring cosmic rays to filter in through the ceiling and interact with the chemistry of the lower atmosphere replicated in the laboratory. "What they found left them agape: a vast number of floating microscopic droplets soon filled the reaction chamber. These were ultra-small clusters of sulfuric acid and water molecules—the building blocks for cloud condensation nuclei—that had been catalyzed by the electrons released by cosmic rays." In effect, *Svensmark's team produced clouds in the laboratory.*

"We were amazed," Svensmark said, "by the speed and efficiency with which the electrons do their work." They had identified a physical mechanism by means of which cosmic rays effectuate earth's cloud cover. But what is the relation to total solar irradiance (TSI)?

Put simply: when the sun emits greater amounts of radiation, its magnetic field is strongest—and protects earth from cosmic ray bombardment. With fewer cosmic rays striking earth's surface, fewer low-lying clouds form, and the cloud cover's cooling effect is thereby removed. The sun's rising TSI directly accounts for only a small percentage of rising earthly temperatures; the removal of significant low-lying cloud cover accounts for a good deal more. Dr. Eugene Parker, one of the world's most accomplished astrophysicists, discoverer of the solar wind, stated about Svensmark's breakthrough:

> ...it is our good fortune that, some years ago, Henrik Svensmark recognized the importance of cloud cover in the temperature control of planet Earth. Svensmark also recognized that the individual water droplets that make up a cloud form mostly where ions have been created by passing cosmic ray particles, thereby tying cloud formation to the varying cosmic ray intensity. That is to say, cosmic rays control the powerful 'cloud valve' that regulates the heating of the earth.

63

Numerous scientists, including Fred Singer in his book, *Unstoppable Global Warming Every 1500 Years*, note the strong correlation between solar variations and earth's changing temperatures. Dr. Singer remarks: "Given the variability of the temperatures, the close correlation between the two is startling." This is important: the current warming trend initiated in the mid-to-late-nineteenth century, prior to any significant rise in atmospheric CO_2 levels; then, in the mid-twentieth century, as CO_2 levels rose, earth's temperatures declined. But the match between solar cycles and earth's varying temperatures, not surprisingly, is close. Put simply: the sun's TSI has been at the high end of its range during the Modern Warm Period, serving as fundamental trigger of rising earthly temperatures.

Repeatedly the IPCC and such prominent political allies as Al Gore make the related claims that astrophysical findings are unrelated to earthly climate change—or, more colloquially: "The sun has nothing to do with it." They generally refuse to debate these issues, claiming either that there is no time for debate, there is time only to act—or that there exists a scientific "consensus" regarding climate change that renders debate unnecessary. Often they refuse to release either their data or methods, even when threatened with lawsuits to be filed under the Freedom of Information Act. Repeatedly they engage in the ad hominem fallacy of personal attack, claiming—rightly or wrongly—that their scientific critics are in the pay of "evil," profit-driven oil companies; i.e., they ignore the arguments and attack the arguers. Often they spew forth invective and claim dissenting scientists are "kooks," outside the mainstream, and/or akin to those who continue to claim the earth is flat—or even to those who deny the Holocaust. The extreme environmentalist accusations are that such scientists are "climate criminals"—and that they should be incarcerated for "crimes against the planet," perhaps even executed.

More damning: the IPCC's "Summary for Policymakers" purports to represent the conclusions reached by 2,500 eminent scientists carefully researching global warming; in fact, the summary is largely written by politicians, not scientists, and, in many cases, contradicts the full report's scientific findings, omitting skepticism regarding AGW claims. It is, of course, the only published IPCC work widely read, reported, cited, or quoted.

Most revealing regarding objectivity and scientific method: the recent "Climategate" scandal exposes leading IPCC scientists seeking to corrupt the peer review process. The dirty trick is to place a crony in position of editorial authority at leading scientific publications; to proceed to publish only papers that tend to support the AGW thesis, and to repudiate those that criticize it; and to then proclaim that the peer-reviewed literature displays "a consensus" supporting the AGW hypothesis. Such "consensus" is achieved by denying access to the technical literature of cutting-edge research and brilliant argumentation performed by many of the world's foremost scientists.

Who stoops to such despicable tactics? Only those who are fiercely committed on emotional grounds to a thesis—and who know that, in fair and open debate, that thesis will be disproven.

Several points must be made.

First: the debate is never over. Regarding any topic, the hallmark of rationality is openness to facts and to logical arguments based in them. A rational individual need not consider arbitrary, data-free, groundless claims—indeed, he must not—but he must be perennially open to new findings, cutting-edge research, and identification of facts previously unknown. Indeed, *the increasingly baleful a crisis, the more imminent looming death, the more urgently is debate required—for the introduction of truthful new evidence might be instrumental in changing course and saving lives.*

Second: The above discussion presents some of the arguments advanced by a handful of the countless superlative scientists critical of the AGW thesis. Even such a brief accounting establishes conclusively that there is no consensus of scientists (or even climate scientists) in support of the AGW cause.

Third: Most important, rational inquiry is not performed by consensus. Truth in science, in philosophy, in any rational discipline is identified by an active, eager, independent mind—examining facts, studying nature. Such a mind is not concerned with what is socially accepted, only with what is. Did Socrates have a consensus behind or opposed to him? Where did the consensus stand regarding Copernicus and Galileo? Or Darwin? Or Pasteur? In the very nature of being an innovative thinker is the overturning of a consensus.

An idea's truth is established by the factual evidence and logical argumentation offered in its support, not by the number of its adherents, even expert adherents. The history of cognition shows that, often, experts are so steeped in their culture's dominant theories and causal explanations that they resist, virtually to the death, revolutionary findings that overturn their core principles, e.g., French scientists in opposition to Pasteur's germ theory of disease. In logic, evidence and reasoning based on such are the decisive factors, not intellectual pedigree; arguments, not the varying accomplishments of the specific arguers. A man of modest intelligence may be right regarding a specific issue, and a genius—or a legion of them—wrong. It is the evidence offered that decides such a question. When a book was published entitled *100 Authors Against Einstein*, the great physicist observed: "If I were wrong, then one would have been enough."

The citation of consensus, rather than evidence, regarding intellectual issues—even where one exists—is invariably an attempt to stifle the independent mind. It is not merely the stuff of politics, rather than science or philosophy, but of totalitarian politics; a method of those who refuse to release their data and/or methods to scientific scrutiny, who refuse to engage in open debate, who misrepresent the conclusions of their own scientists, who simply ignore countervailing research and evidence, who shamelessly engage in hysterical scare-mongering, who employ cronyism to deny critics access to the scientific journals, and who seek to shove virulent statism down the throats of millions of free men in alleged attempt to ameliorate a threat they know to be bogus. Such methods are inherently emotionalist, coercive, and anti-intellectual—and are utterly inappropriate to serious scientific and/or philosophical debate.

If this were not enough, there exist other significant objections to IPCC charges and proposed solutions. One is the truth that warming temperatures are generally beneficial to life on earth, not harmful. Examples supporting this conclusion abound: (1) During the Medieval Warm Period, Norse colonies prospered even on Greenland. (2) Vegetative life flourishes in warmer climes and in the consequent rising levels of atmospheric CO_2, which supports the process of photosynthesis essential to plant life. Crops are more readily grown, with the result of increasing food supply. (3) The earth, generally much warmer throughout its past, has sustained tropical life forms near its polar regions. Although scorching temperatures can be as lethal as frigid ones, it is earth's warmer periods of recent millennia—not colder ones—that enhanced life. For example, the declining temperatures of the Little Ice Age wrecked the Norse Greenland settlements; similarly, and on a considerably grander scale, remorselessly advancing ice sheets crushed or drove before them all life forms during earth's ice ages.

Further, what will enable human beings to best adapt to earth's ever-shifting climate? We reside in the midst of an ice age's warm interglacial period—but, in time, the ice will return with the planet's inevitably declining temperatures. Can man prevent it? If not, what factor(s) will promote most effectual adaptation? Certainly mankind's best hope for eliminating, or foreshortening, or surviving extreme climate changes are the advances in science, technology, and industrialization that, for example, make it possible to grow crops in colder climes—and/or predict coming cataclysms—and/or evacuate millions in the face of catastrophe—and/or create medications to cure (or treat) ailments generated, in part, by extreme weather conditions—and/or construct powerful dams and levees—and/or create technologies as inconceivable today as were jet planes, nuclear plants, and the Internet centuries ago; technologies that might benefit man's life in the face of pronounced climate change in ways equally unimaginable today.

A scale back of applied science, technology, and industrialization makes man immensely more susceptible—not less so—to the dangers of extreme climate change, while doing absolutely zero to prevent such natural variations.

Any current attempt—including cap and trade—to coercively diminish deployment of fossil fuels massively undermines man's technological and industrial development, and thereby perpetrates even worse consequences than severely diminishing men's living standards. It leaves them—like our ancestors—gravely crippled in ability to respond to such natural calamities as drought, flood, storm, earthquake, volcano, plague, inexorably advancing ice sheets, and devastating asteroid/comet impact.

The insanity of the AGW claims and proposed solutions were eloquently summed up by Richard Lindzen, Professor of Atmospheric Sciences at the Massachusetts Institute of Technology (MIT), and former lead writer for the IPCC. Dr. Lindzen stated: "Future generations will wonder in bemused amazement that the early twenty-first century's developed world went into hysterical panic over a globally averaged temperature increase of a few tenths of a degree, and, on the basis of gross exaggerations of highly uncertain computer projections combined into implausible chains of inference, proceeded to contemplate a roll-back of the industrial age."

The claim of man-made global warming is not a scientific theory. It is a sham theory advanced by politicians, political journalists, and shamelessly politicized "scientists"; advanced to promote and enforce a philosophy of nature's intrinsic value, an ethic of human sacrifice to the sacredness of nonhuman nature, and a politics of an environmental police state. As solely a component of an utterly false

67

and death-dealing philosophy, it is to be contemptuously dismissed in favor of a philosophy thoroughly life giving.

Here is a proper "Summary for Policymakers": Recognize that environmentalist restrictions on industrialization, energy development, and economic growth proceed from delusions generated by a profoundly irrational philosophy, not from scientific data. Man-made global warming is, at best, a myth; at worst, a hoax. Proposed cap and trade legislation is a rights-violating, economy-crushing policy grounded solely in profound intellectual aberration; as such, it must be disdainfully repudiated. Claims that technological advance exacerbate, rather than reduce air and water pollution, are a canard. Belief that industrial civilization represents man's departure from or rejection of nature is a lethal philosophic error.

If you venerate human life on earth—and if you do not, you have no business making policy—you must embrace the freedom of the capitalist system that liberates mankind's best thinkers. Such minds will create the next wave of technology that will further elevate living standards and life expectancies—in a manner similar to that accomplished by electricity, telephones, oil production, nuclear power, steel, automobiles, airplanes, antibiotics, computers, and the Internet.

The main moral issue in human life, as ever, is: the freedom of man's mind.

2

Defeating Islamic Totalitarianism

Three-and-a-half years after a brutal assault on American forces at Pearl Harbor—by the summer of 1945—Japanese military power had been crushed. The Japanese fleet had been sunk, their planes blasted from the skies, their empire torn from their grasp, their homeland ringed by an invincible armada. A remorseless, implacable America prepared to deliver a death blow to the country's fanatically militaristic regime.

By contrast, today, *nine years* after a brutal assault on American civilians in New York City and Washington, DC—by the fall of 2010—the power of the Islamist enemy grows ominously. Various fanatical sects are actively engaged in jihad: they assail U.S. forces in Afghanistan—wreak bloody terrorist violence around the world, including in the United States, e.g., the Fort Hood massacre—inculcate virulent anti-Western hatred in mosques and madrassahs—support such murderous terrorist organizations as Hezbollah, Al Qaeda, Hamas, and others—and, in Iran, develop nuclear weapons.

What is the primary cause of such monumental differences in outcome? What principle explains America's smashing success in World War II—and embarrassing failure in the current conflict?

Before answering the question, it is wise to identify one factor that is not a cause: America's military strength relative to that of its enemies.

The Axis Powers of World War II—National Socialist Germany, Imperial Japan, Fascist Italy, and, for a time, Soviet Russia—constituted an immensely powerful military alliance. Germany and Japan especially had been built on war economies, actively preparing for years to launch wars of conquest. Both countries possessed powerful armies that swept opposition before them, mighty navies featuring numerous aircraft carriers and/or the seas' most formidable battleships, significant air power, and a military backed by technologically and industrially advanced societies. The United States, by contrast, on the eve of her entry into World War II, was an industrial powerhouse (although mired in the Great Depression)—but, militarily, woefully unprepared. It took crash programs from the war's inception to raise, train, and arm a military capable of defeating Fascism.

But in 2001 and the years following, America's enemies were and remain laughably weak regarding military power. The Islamists possess no long-distance missiles or nuclear warheads with which to obliterate American cities—they have no planes to strafe or bomb U.S. forces—no armies capable of opposing America's military. They cannot fight tiny Israel on equal military terms, let alone America—and do not even try; rather, they detonate homemade bombs in populated civilian areas—and, incapable of creating jet aircraft, steal them to deploy as weapons. Worse, for them, their economies are tyrannically oppressed and impoverished, their cultures dominated by dark-age religion, and their scientific, technological, and industrial development stands at nil. The Islamists are pitifully backward in every conceivable form. The Americans must even develop the oil fields that provide the wealth necessary to execute jihad.

In contrast, America, the world's lone superpower, is immensely freer, vastly more advanced, enormously wealthier, and stupendously more powerful. In the words of historian, John Lewis: "In our own day, the technological and industrial superiority of the U.S. over the Middle East is staggering. Islamic warriors can shoot an AK-47, but they cannot build one; all of the arms possessed by Islamic countries come from outside those countries. They are pathetically weak; the American army ended the regime of Saddam Hussein in three weeks, after Iran could not beat him in *eight years.*"

Were America willing to use its full military might against the Islamists, this would be a short and decisive conflict, indeed—significantly shorter and just as definitive as her victory over Japan. Why would not she do it? Why does she not crush her enemies—as she did sixty-five years ago—in self-defense? Why does her government leave American civilians in mortal peril from jihadist attack? What holds her back?

Some people believe that because America faced national governments in World War II, the enemy was less difficult to locate, engage, and defeat; and because she faces rootless, state-less terror organizations today, the prospect is dauntingly difficult. This is false. For example, when Hezbollah butchered 241 U.S. Marines in Beirut in

1983, the location of its bases in Lebanon were well known. But President Reagan's response was to pull U.S. forces from Lebanon—not to obliterate the foe. Further, it is no secret which governments finance, arm, and support Hezbollah—those of Syria and Iran. But the United States takes no military action to destroy those regimes.

The full answer to the above questions lies in modern philosophy. But begin with telling details and then build to wider principles—begin with the difference in tactics. President Roosevelt identified the enemy as Fascism, asked for and received a declaration of war, pronounced the enemy's unconditional surrender the only acceptable outcome, and waged unremitting, all-out war to achieve it. Franklin Delano Roosevelt's (FDR) successor, President Truman, dropped the atomic bomb—twice—on Japanese cities to ensure such a result.

By contrast, President Bush refused to identify the enemy, labeled his military campaigns a "War on Terror," neither requested nor received a declaration of war, and waged half-assed wars, with debilitating rules of engagement, against two countries who were not the main enemy, leaving the primary foe—Iran—physically unscathed; indeed, strengthened by the overthrow of its main regional enemy—the regime of Saddam Hussein.

What must be done? First, identify the enemy—second, specify the intended outcome—third, use all necessary means to achieve it.

The enemy today is: Islamic Totalitarianism. Terrorism is not an enemy. It is a tactic of warfare employed by a foe too weak to defeat us militarily. By analogy, imagine that FDR did not identify the foe as Fascism, but rather, labeled his campaigns a "War on the Blitzkrieg," a favored Nazi tactic.

Further, the terrorists attacking our cities and murdering our civilians are not everyday thugs, seeking unearned loot. Nor are they secular activists, enraged by so-called "American imperialism," seeking redress for specific political/economic injustices. (For example, the regimes they support—those of the Taliban and the Iranian mullahs—are, in accordance with the jihadists' own moral principles, far more murderously brutal than America's enemies accuse her of being.) They are religious zealots, seeking to establish a global Islamist theocratic dictatorship, similar to that in Iran. Whether Sunni or Shiite, Al Qaeda or Hezbollah et al., the Islamist goal remains constant: the founding of theocracies in which *sharia*, Islamic Law, becomes the law of the land—first in Middle Eastern states, then around the globe. Do most Muslims support this cause?

Probably not, hopefully not; but some sizeable subset—known today as Islamists—does.

But totalitarian religion, not Fascism or Communism or any other secular cause, is the ideology driving our enemies.

Abu Bakar Ba'asyir, a teacher at an Islamic school, and a murderer convicted in the 2002 Bali bombing, then released from prison in 2006, stated the Islamist motivation forthrightly. He spoke specifically of Indonesia, but in terms representative of Islamists everywhere: "We demand an Islamic state, and not some form of Islamisation of society. *We want the state to be Islamic*, with Islamic leaders who have the courage and will to implement the Islamic law in total...There is no space and no room for democratic consultation. The Islamic law is set and fixed, so why discuss it? Just implement it!" (Emphasis added.)

This is exactly what the ayatollahs in Iran, for example, have done. Elan Journo, in his excellent book, *Winning The Unwinnable War*, noted: "Domestically, using radios, billboards, posters, school text-books, postage stamps, currency—through every medium—the clerics worked to reshape the society according to Islamic dictates." There was no "democratic consultation," no individual choice, no freedom to disagree. People accepted and obeyed Islamic law—or were severely punished. Iranian authors and journalists who dissented, for example, were executed, among them Ali Dashti, tortured in Iranian prison—despite his age of eighty-plus years—for writings critical of Islam. This must be emphasized: *thousands of Iranians* have been executed by the regime for merely expressing thoughts critical of their religion.

In February 1989, Iranian spiritual and political leader, Ayatollah Ruhollah Khomeini, issued an infamous *fatwa*, calling for the assassination of Indian author, Salman Rushdie, whose book, *Satanic Verses*, disparaged Islam.

In his public declaration, Khomeini stated: "I would like to inform all the intrepid Muslims in the world that the author of the book entitled *Satanic Verses*...as well as those publishers who were aware of its contents, are hereby sentenced to death. I call on all zealous Muslims to execute them quickly, wherever they find them, so that no one will dare to insult Islamic sanctity." Khomeini proceeded to place a $5 million bounty on Rushdie's head. It must be pointed out that Rushdie was an English—not an Iranian—citizen; and the publishers "sentenced to death," English and American.

Khomeini never hid the goal of either his regime or, more broadly, of the Islamist movement. "The governments of the world," he stated, "should know that Islam cannot be defeated. Islam will be victorious in all the countries of the world, and Islam and the teachings of the Koran will prevail all over the world." America's Islamist enemies are open regarding their stated goals: the establishment of political Islam—of totalitarian religion—first in states of the Arab-Islamic world, and then across the globe.

The jihadists hold a philosophy based on their interpretation of Islam's fundamental texts: the Koran, held as an infallible source of God's revealed word—the Hadith or Traditions, a compendium of sayings and actions ascribed to Mohammed—and the sira, the earliest biographies of The Prophet, considered authoritatively accurate. Unfortunately, the jihadists' interpretation has abundant supporting evidence in such works; their militant philosophy of global domination is not arrant, aberrant misinterpretation of their religion's cardinal tenets—such a goal is inextricably among them.

The Koran, be it remembered, according to Muslims, is the direct word of God. Allah, through the angel Gabriel, dictated its every thought and syllable to Mohammed. The Koran is, according to Islamic belief—in the words of historian, Robert Spencer—"a perfect copy of an eternal book…that has existed forever with Allah." Unlike in Christianity, there is no distinction in Islam between fundamentalist and nonfundamentalist interpretations of the holy book—because there are no nonfundamentalist interpretations of the Koran. According to Islamic teaching, the "perfect copy of an eternal book" must be taken literally. And what does the book teach? Following are several excerpts that contain only a part—but an undeniable part—of its message:

> "[F]ight and slay the unbelievers wherever you find them, seize them, beleaguer them, and lie in wait for them in every stratagem of war; but if they repent, and practice our way, then accept them." (9:5). Or: "O True believers, when you encounter the unbelievers, strike off their heads." (47:4). Or: "You shall fight back against those who do not believe in God, nor in the Last Day, nor do they prohibit what God and his messenger have prohibited, nor do they abide by the religion of truth." (9:29). To those who prefer peace to bloody conquest, the holy book states: "If you do not fight, He will punish you severely, and put others in your place." (9:39). Why should true Muslims war against nonbelievers? The Koran's answer, in multiple locations, is unequivocal: "God's curse be upon the infidels!" (2:89). "God is the enemy of the unbelievers." (2: 98). "Theirs shall be a woeful punishment." (2:175.) Etc.

Nor is such exhortation to holy warfare mere theory; it is deeply embodied by Islamic practice dating to the religion's earliest days. This point is borne out by Mohammed's life—and by the homage paid to him. The Koran states: "Ye have indeed in the Messenger of Allah a beautiful pattern [alternatively an 'excellent model'] of conduct for any one whose hope is in Allah and the Final Day..." (33:21). For almost 1,400 years Muslims have been (and continue to be) exhorted to hold Mohammed as an archetype of proper behavior. Robert Spencer stated: "The Qur'an and Islamic tradition are clear that the Prophet is the supreme example of behavior for Muslims to follow."

And what were Mohammed's actions like? That The Prophet could be kind and generous is beyond dispute; it is established in abundant Islamic sources. At the same time, however, Mohammed was, in large part, a bloody-handed conqueror, emphatically different from Jesus; a point authenticated by the most authoritative compiler of *ahadith*—Bukhari (810–870)—and by The Prophet's most honored (by Muslims) biographer: Ibn Ishaq (704–773); in addition to numerous other respected Islamic sources.

The man Muslims are universally urged to emulate was—among other things—a warrior who counseled, planned, led, and fought in jihad over a period of years. For example, the above-named sources tell us that in leading a raid on the Quraysh, his own tribe turned enemy, Mohammed told his followers, "no man will be slain this day fighting against them with steadfast courage advancing not retreating but God will cause him to enter Paradise." Spencer noted that this is a promise "that has given heart to Muslim warriors throughout the ages."

Mohammed ordered the assassination of the poet, Ka'b bin Al-Ashraf, who allegedly composed verses critical of Muslim women, and praised God when the murder was successfully completed. The Prophet led Muslim forces into battle at Uhud. After defeating an enemy tribe, the Banu Qurayzah, he sanctioned and participated in the massacre of its warrior-prisoners; personally aiding in their decapitation. Upon seizing wealth of a subjugated hostile tribe, the Banu Nadir, Mohammed—an abstemious man of modest tastes—spent on himself only what was necessary for his family, and, according to a most reliable compiler of hadith, "would spend what remained for purchasing horses and weapons as preparation for Jihad." He conquered Mecca as part of such holy war, shortly after most of Arabia, and called for similar religious conquest far beyond its borders. (He also, at age fifty-two, married Aisha, aged seven, consummated the marriage when she was nine, and, *being an exemplar of model conduct*, remains among pious Muslims to this day the inspiration for similar marriages to child brides.)

That the barbaric practices of a seventh-century religious conqueror are still upheld—by hundreds of millions—as a moral archetype is, in itself, a truth deeply disturbing.

The logic is remorselessly, terrifyingly inescapable: Mohammed was a warrior, killer, and aggressive conqueror in the name of God—Muslims are relentlessly exhorted to emulate his holy example—some Muslims, therefore, are warriors, killers, and aggressive conquerors in the name of God. The Koran states: "He who obeys the Messenger, obeys Allah." (4:80).

Ibn Warraq, author of a courageous testimonial to religious freedom, *Why I Am Not a Muslim*, was unfortunately correct: Islamists possess far more religious legitimacy supporting their calls for holy war than do rational Muslims supporting their calls for peace. As Spencer made the point: "It is difficult, if not impossible, to maintain that Islam is a religion of peace when warfare and booty were among the chief preoccupations of the Prophet of Islam."

The respected *Dictionary of Islam* defines "jihad" as: "a religious war with those who are unbelievers in the mission of Mohammed. It is an incumbent religious duty, established in the Koran and in the Traditions [Hadith] as a divine institution, enjoined specially for the purpose of advancing Islam..." Ibn Warraq, writing from extensive knowledge of Islamic tradition, observes: "It is a grave sin for a Muslim to shirk the battle against the unbelievers—those who do will roast in Hell...It is abundantly clear from many...verses that the Koran is not talking of metaphorical battles or of moral crusades: it is talking of the battlefield."

Sam Harris stated in his book, *The End of Faith*: "On almost every page the Koran instructs observant Muslims to despise non-believers. On almost every page, it prepares the ground for religious conflict." Ibn Warraq points out: "We must take seriously what the Islamists say to understand their motivation that it is the divinely ordained duty of all Muslims to fight in the literal sense until man-made law has been replaced by God's law, the sharia, and Islamic law has conquered the entire world...For every text the liberal Muslims produce, the mullahs will use dozens of counter-examples [that are] exegetically, philosophically, historically far more legitimate."

For example, Khomeini stated: "Islam makes it incumbent on all adult males, provided they are not disabled and incapacitated, to prepare themselves for the conquest of [other] countries so that the writ of Islam is obeyed in every country in the world...Those who know nothing of Islam pretend that Islam counsels against war. Those [who say this] are witless. Islam says: Kill all the unbelievers just as they would kill you." The profoundly intractable problem is that such beliefs are not idiosyncratic personal insanities peculiar to Iranian mullahs and their specific followers; but are deeply embedded in the earliest, most authoritative Islamic sources, including the hallowed activities of the ideal man.

Why? By now, the answer is manifest: Islam is the one true faith; its revelations perfect and supersede those of the Bible. As such it is a holy religious obligation of Muslims to bring Islam to all human beings. Humanity is thereby sundered into two groups: Muslims and non-Muslims. True Muslims reside in the Dar al-Islam—the Land of Islam—where the faith's basic tenets are properly obeyed; non-Muslims inhabit the Dar al-Harb—the Land of Warfare—and such infidel lands are fated to become Islamic by either conversion or conquest. Ibn Warraq pointed out: "All acts of war are permitted in the Dar al-Harb."

The English meaning of the word "Islam" is: *submission.*

Two terrifying truths emerge from such considerations. One: the Islamists construe their religion's core teachings (and model behaviors) as exhortation to impose *sharia* on the world's human population by pitiless, even murderous force. Stated Khomeini: "Islam says: Whatever good there is exists thanks to the sword...People cannot be made obedient except with the sword." Two: unfortunately, the jihadists have ample supporting evidence for such conclusions in the Koran, the Hadith, and the sira.

The Islamists are true to their principles. Their fundamental texts predominantly—perhaps overwhelmingly—enjoin them to compel all men, in all lands, to submit to *sharia.* This is what they seek to accomplish. And always have.

For example, after The Prophet's death in 632 AD, his father-in-law and trusted lieutenant, Abu Bakr, ascended to power and sustained Mohammed's jihadist mission: he established the caliphate, consolidated Muslim power in Arabia, invaded the Persian and Byzantine Empires, and conquered present-day Syria and Iraq. Early Islamists proceed to subjugate large swathes of the globe.

During the same period, jihadist fervor against the West helped fuel aggressive conquest by various Muslim factions. For example, Arab and Berber warriors conquered Spain in 711 AD, held much of the country for a full five centuries, and were not finally expelled until 1492. (According to Islamic teaching, a land, once Muslim, remains so forever; therefore, Spain still belongs to Islam.) They crossed the Pyrenees and invaded France, but were defeated by Charles Martel, grandfather of Charlemagne, in 732 at the Battle of Tours. In 827, Arab warriors invaded Sicily, and, after decades of hard fighting, finally conquered the island in 902. For almost two hundred years they held dominion, until finally expelled by Norman knights in 1091.

In the Middle East, Muslim armies were a virtually irresistible force. Egyptian-born scholar, Bat Ye-or, observed: "Led by brilliant and fearless leaders, the Muslims overcame the Persian armies and seized Babylonia, Susiana, Mesopotamia, Armenia, and Persia, pushing on as far as the Sind [in present day Pakistan]...In the West, they conquered all the Christian provinces of the eastern Mediterranean, from Syria and Palestine, to Egypt, North Africa and through Spain..." These conquests were accompanied by unspeakable atrocities remorselessly perpetrated on civilian populations, including clergymen. "The monasteries were pillaged, the monks killed, and Monophysite [Christian] Arabs massacred, enslaved, or Islamized by force."

For centuries, such Islamic aggression against the Byzantine Empire was so pervasive that, finally, in the eleventh century the Byzantine Emperor, by now Orthodox, not Catholic—and condemning the popes as schismatic—nevertheless appealed to the West for help. In response, in 1095 Pope Urban II at the Council of Clermont called for what became the First Crusade. The pope was, in the words of Robert Spencer, "calling for a defensive action—one that was long overdue." Given that Muslims had militarily conquered vast swathes of formerly Christian dominions, slaughtered Christians—both clergy and laymen—destroyed numerous churches, and threatened pilgrims to the Holy Land, Spencer's description of the First Crusade as "a defensive action...long overdue" is accurate.

Middle-East scholar, Bernard Lewis, wrote of the one thousand-year dominance the Muslims enjoyed over Christianity, a mastery achieved "since the advent of Islam in the seventh century and the irruption of the Muslim armies from Arabia into the then Christian lands of Syria, Palestine, Egypt, North Africa, and, for awhile, Southern Europe. The Crusaders had briefly halted the triumphal march of Islam, but they had been held, defeated, and ejected. The Muslim advance had continued with the extinction of Byzantium and the Ottoman entry into Europe."

It is difficult for modern Westerners, born into a world for three centuries dominated by Western Civilization, to appreciate (or even vaguely remember) that the Islamic Middle East was immensely superior to Europe in every important cultural manifestation, emphatically including military conquest, for a full millennium from the seventh century through the seventeenth.

In time, the Turks, not the Arabs, became the primary ethnic group driving jihad against Europe. One central example not widely known in contemporary America—but crying for awareness—involves the Ottoman siege of Vienna in 1683. The Turks, in the form of the Ottoman Empire, had become the dominant Islamic power of the day. They conquered Constantinople, capital of the Byzantine Empire in 1453, carved out an immense empire in the Middle East and North Africa, and conquered most of Eastern and Central Europe, which they occupied for centuries. Twice they laid siege to Vienna. In late summer of 1683, as they mounted their second and last siege, they were soundly and decisively thrashed by the relieving army of John Sobieski, King John III of Poland. The climactic battle took place on September 12, 1683.

The siege was, in effect, the last hurrah for the Ottoman Empire. It slowly weakened thereafter—endless wars of liberation beset it in Eastern Europe—and Western Europe, on the cusp of its Enlightenment era, soon supplanted it as the major power in the world. (Eventually, it was crushed in World War I, but not before its dying spasm slaughtered roughly 1.5 million innocent Armenian Christians, a holocaust that served as model for the later Nazi genocide, and one that, to this day, is denied by the Turkish Government.) Vienna is, geographically, roughly halfway between Constantinople (by then Istanbul) and London, a fact demonstrating how much of Europe the Turks had conquered and threatened. But, after the lifting of the second siege of Vienna—no longer. Jihad, once so feared throughout Europe, was diminishing, supplanted by a long era of Western dominance.

The crushing September 12th defeat at Vienna can be realistically viewed as the beginning of the end of centuries of Ottoman military dominance.

September 11, 1683, therefore represents the historical high point of the jihad against the West.

Did Osama bin Laden pick the date of September 11th from a hat? He did not. He chose it to make a grand historic gesture. His murderous actions—and the date deliberately chosen—stated, in effect: "Jihad, for centuries quiescent, is back. Be afraid. Be very afraid."

Historians point out that much of the endless aggression perpetrated by Muslim regimes may be explained simply as "good, old-fashioned imperialism," irrespective of religion. This may well be true, as naked power lust is a moral ailment that afflicts men of all cultures. Nevertheless, when a Muslim ruler sought to conquer lands of the infidel, he invariably appealed to jihad—sincerely or not—and generally found immense support from both clergy and populace.

Since Islam requires conquest of the globe, jihad is not directed exclusively against the West but, even more aggressively, against the non-Judaic-Christian East. Unlike Jews and Christians, monotheists, "People of the Book"—the Bible—and guardians of true albeit imperfect earlier revelations, Hindus were regarded as pagans deserving of no protection under Islamic law. Consequently, they were exterminated by the tens of millions. Francois Gautier, in *Rewriting Indian History*, wrote: "Invaders, who believed in one God, came upon this country which had a million gods...And for them it was the symbol of all they thought was wrong. So the genocide...which was perpetrated was tremendous." Indian historian, Sita Ram Goel, stated: "Islamic imperialism...required its warriors to fall upon the helpless civil population...in mass murders of non-combatants...they did all this as *mujahids* (holy warriors) and *ghazis* (unbeliever-killers) in the service of Allah and his Last Prophet."

Indian historian K.S. Lal estimated that "the Hindu population decreased by *eighty million* between 1000 [AD] and 1525...probably the biggest holocaust in the world's history." (Emphasis added.) Regardless the specific number of innocent lives claimed, eminent American historian, Will Durant, concurred with Lal's overall assessment: "The Islamic conquest of India is probably the bloodiest story in history."

Indeed, it may well be plausible to conclude that Arabic Muslims are the most successful imperialists of history. They militarily conquered and permanently imposed their religious culture on vast regions populated by multiple advanced civilizations: Christians of the Middle East and North Africa, Zoroastrians of ancient Persia, Hindus of India. Immense numbers of present-day Muslims are raised to accept a culture, language, and faith brutally imposed on their ancestors. They accept a religion, in Ibn Warraq's words that "originated thousands

79

of miles away, [they learn] to read a book in a language that they do not understand, which they learn to read and write before they know their mother tongue or the national language." Indian writer, V.S. Naipaul, noted: "The time before Islam is a time of blackness: that is part of Muslim theology. History has to serve theology." The result is that numberless millions of Muslims learn the history, culture, and religion of their conquerors and not the glories of their own earlier civilizations *prior to* the coerced imposition of Islam. "Bowing toward Arabia five times a day," observed Warraq, "must surely be the ultimate symbol of this cultural imperialism."

Worst of all: the religion forced on their ancestors is the one true faith; conversion to another, or overt abandonment of it in any form, represents the heinous crime of apostasy—assessed more abominable than murder—and punished by death; as is any open criticism of the faith, its holy book, and/or its prophet. Jihadists of a millennium gone by conquered the ancestors of most contemporary Muslims, and jihadists today continue to hold in thrall the minds—and lives—of their descendants.

Islamic Totalitarianism dominates vast portions of the globe and has done so for centuries. The modern jihad of the past 30 years is but its logical continuation.

Muslims, holding theirs as the one perfected faith, were accustomed to centuries of cultural superiority and military conquest; afterall, God understandably favored them. The cultural rise of the West, and history's reversal of military fortune in the form of European imperialism, left them with no answer to a profound question: Why did God now accord dominion to the infidel? Or, as Bernard Lewis entitled his book on this theme, "What went wrong?" It was right in every sense, preeminently moral, for holy warriors to hold sway over non-believers; equally wrong for the reverse. As late as the seventeenth century, and perhaps even beyond, Lewis pointed out that in the heart of the Islamic world: "they were still inclined to dismiss the denizens of the lands beyond the Western frontier as benighted barbarians...It was a judgment that had for long been reasonably accurate. It was becoming dangerously out of date."

Western incursions into sacred Islamic homelands, including the 1948 establishment of the state of Israel, were inevitably construed as monstrously wrong—a desecration—an inversion of a fitting East–West relation—and profoundly intolerable. Simply put: the one perfected religion merits proper hegemony over subordinate faiths and degraded cultures; a reversal of this natural (or supernatural) order flouts God's command. Inevitably, Islamists are outraged by such monumental injustice and seek, in multiple forms, including mass murder, to restore to a world turned topsy-turvy the rectitude of God's will.

It is eminently logical that if a specific religion is the "one true faith," and all other ideologies mere pretenders, then a colossal double standard regarding imperialism—even cultural influence—would follow: God mandates the true religion's cultural, even military, dominance of the infidel; and anathematizes the infidel's dominance of the true religion. Bat Ye'or wrote: "Jihad is central to Islamic history and civilization...Neither American policy nor Israel's perversity have bred this hostility; it is nourished by a culture of aversion toward, and hatred of, infidels." Allah, in the form of His one finalized, perfected message, must reign universally supreme.

That Arab–Islamic culture was, for several centuries, one of the glories of mankind's history—and, hopefully, will one day be so again—is a clear historical fact; unfortunately, this truth in no way vitiates the terrifying reality that Islamic teachings encourage, indeed require, aggressive conquest of the Dar al-Harb.

Readers may ask themselves: If they sought to establish a global Islamist theocracy, who or what constitutes the principal impediment? Western Civilization in general—and the United States in particular. America is the world's freest nation, the one in which the principle of individual rights was most deeply embodied, where religious freedom was first instituted and consistently upheld, and where establishment of an official state religion, to which all must submit, is constitutionally prohibited.

Further, it is where capitalism achieved its full fruition; the country where making money, earning success, pursuing happiness—*earthly* happiness—are the ruling values. This country—above all its creed of individual rights and material prosperity—is the ideological enemy. Individuals there bow neither to Mecca nor before the clergy; their lives belong not to God, but to themselves; they seek wealth, not salvation; and they accept or reject religious belief as they deem fit, with no fear of reprisal from a theocratic state. Such values mark America as an inveterately secular society and implacable foe of totalitarian religion; indeed, as Khomeini labeled her, "The Great Satan"—an epithet all Americans should proudly embrace.

And because America was the freest country, because it most consistently upheld and protected an individual's right to his own life, it was the most willing and able to defend itself. Western Europeans, excluding the British, defended themselves ineffectually against the Fascists; relied on America to defend them from the Soviets; and, today, cower abysmally before the Islamists. But Americans will no more take orders from Khomeini than they will from Hitler or Stalin. The United States was overwhelmingly responsible for defeating National Socialist Germany; virtually single-handedly vanquished Imperial Japan; and, as the Free World's lone super power, shielded it from Communist tyranny. Similarly, if the Free World is to be saved from Islamist aggression, America will be its primary, perhaps exclusive bulwark. America can and will defend itself—and the Islamists know sufficient history to recognize this truth.

If a global Islamist state is to be transformed from vision into reality, its main foe, the United States of America, *the Great Satan*, must be assailed and destroyed. As stated by Benjamin Netanyahu, a leading international expert regarding Islamist terrorism: "...establishing a resurgent Islam requires not merely rolling back the West [from the Middle East]; it requires destroying its main engine, the United States. And if the United States cannot be destroyed just now, it can be... ferociously attacked again and again, until it is brought to its knees. But the ultimate goal remains...[d]estroy America and win eternity." Netanyahu's statement needs amending regarding but one important particular: The Islamists seek to establish sharia on earth—across the globe—in addition to winning eternity, i.e., gaining salvation.

Which individual, group, or state is the primary promulgator of such jihad against America?

Since the Khomeini Revolution of 1979, the world leader of jihad, in every conceivable form, is unquestionably the Islamic Republic of Iran. The regime of the ayatollahs is, simultaneously, the main instigator and supporter of Islamist terrorist assaults on Americans—and, more fundamentally, is the ideological fountainhead of modern jihad.

In terms of violent physical assault, the regime was virtually birthed in attack on America: the seizure of the U.S. embassy in Tehran in 1979 and the forced captivity of American hostages for well over a year. Several years subsequent, the mullahs were behind the afore-mentioned bombing of Marine barracks in Lebanon—"the single deadliest attack for U.S. Marines since the battle of Iwo Jima." FBI investigation into the bombing of Khobar Towers in Saudi Arabia in 1996—an attack killing seventeen Americans—identified the Iranians as those behind it.

The 9/11 Commission found that senior Al Qaeda agents journeyed to Iran for training in explosives, and that at least eight of the fourteen Saudi hijackers traveled to and from Iran between October 2000 and February 2001. The Iranian regime regularly hosts conferences for international terrorist organizations, and has been labeled by the U.S. State department the "most active state sponsor of terrorism." For three decades, Iran has waged lethal proxy war against America.

More fundamentally, the Khomeini Revolution and the establishment of a militantly aggressive Islamist regime in Iran provided the ideological foundation of modern jihad—jihad that had lain dormant, but not extinct, for three centuries. In overthrowing a secular, Western-backed regime, by humiliating America via the hostage crisis, in openly, aggressively broadcasting jihadist goals—by integrating violent rhetoric with bloody deed—Khomeini's regime fanned the flames of an Islamist movement, inspiring would-be jihadists across the globe.

In the words of Elan Journo, the Khomeini Revolution "proved to followers of the movement that their ideal was achievable. The truly pious could, in fact, prevail over the materially more powerful infidels and apostates." Pictures of Khomeini appeared in Egypt and, eventually, across the Islamic world. The militant Egyptian group, Al-Jihad, headed by Ayman al-Zawahiri, subsequently bin Laden's lieutenant in Al Qaeda, produced leaflets and tapes urging other Islamic organizations to emulate the Iranians. One commentator wrote: "Iranian revolution contributed to a revival of the political role of mosques in the mobilization of politically-oriented Islamic elements throughout the Islamic world."

The Muslim Brotherhood, founded in Egypt in 1928, seeking to overthrow secular regimes to be replaced by theocracies imposing sharia, was galvanized by events in Iran. Adherents "frequently cited the Iranian revolution as evidence of the eventual victory of those who followed the path of God." In Palestine, the Iranian victory led to the conviction that the time for jihad was now: the terror organization Palestinian Islamic Jihad broke away from the Muslim Brotherhood, and quoted as inspiration a Khomeini fatwa stating that annihilating the "'Zionist entity' is a religious duty." As Journo stated: "Eventually the Muslim Brotherhood spun off its own jihadist outfit—Hamas—to lead the revived campaign against Israel." So the madness went, on it goes at accelerating pace, and on it will continue to accelerate, so long as America takes no steps to expunge it.

But is war necessary? Cannot the Islamists be reasoned with? Afterall, like us, they are human beings. Are they not open to honest negotiation?

All rational human beings abhor and seek to avoid the appalling bloodshed of war. They properly seek resolution of grievances via negotiation, not obliteration. The death struggle against Fascism, for example—the round-the-clock rain of death on German cities, the fire bombing of Dresden and Tokyo, the nuclear assault on Hiroshima and Nagasaki—can innocent human beings, whose lives span decades of uninterrupted peace, and who hold no first-hand encounter with such events of Hell, even imagine the unspeakable horror of blowing to pieces, or incinerating, children and babies among numberless other innocent civilians? Current Americans received a taste of such madness on 9/11—and recoiled in outrage and dread. It is worth a great deal—but not any price—to evade such devastation.

Can the Islamists be negotiated with? It would be an immense boon to humanity if it were so. But is it?

After the above discussion, it is clear that America's current enemies are consistent in both word and deed, theory and practice; therefore, in terms of overall goal and strategy, eminently predictable. Theirs is the one glittering jewel-faith whose radiance must suffuse the globe. It must gain rightful dominion over the world's populace.

And if, for sundry reasons, men reject it? They must be assailed, conquered, killed—until the rest submit. "People cannot be made obedient except with the sword"—or the bomb. It is blasphemy to subordinate the jewel faith to lesser religions, or to secularism, or to nonbelievers of any creed; there may be no co-existence with false gods; the single true faith must universally reign; Islam must be catholic. The brutal truth is that Islamists now—and for 1,400 prior years—offer(ed) to infidels a series of stark, limited alternatives: conversion to Islam—or subjugation in dhimmitude, i.e., as second-class citizens, legally oppressed in a state governed by sharia—or warfare until submission in one of the first two forms is achieved. *No other options are offered.* These were the only three choices presented to unbelievers by The Prophet—and his divinely inspired example is to be unalterably emulated.

A negotiated settlement, in which each party respects the right of the other to live peacefully in accordance with its fundamental principles, regardless of philosophic/religious difference—*absent submission to Islam in some form*—is out of the question. Bat Ye-or reminded us: "As the jihad is *a permanent war*, it excludes the idea of peace but authorizes temporary truces..." regarding struggles in which Muslims are currently too weak to prevail. (Emphasis added.)

For a full millennium the West properly feared jihad. But men's memories are short, and the swirl of changing events and eras often mutes them. The rise of Western Europe (and their North American colonies) during the Enlightenment period and its aftermath was driven by burgeoning respect for the individual—for his right to his own life and to his own mind. The growing political/economic free-dom of the capitalist period liberated the great creative minds of the Western world, and led to immense achievements in philosophy, the arts, theoretical and applied science, technology, and an industrial revolution.

A philosophic counter-revolution, spearheaded in Germany by such thinkers as Hegel and Marx, building on a Kantian foundation, rejected egoism and individualism—repudiated any principle of a man's inalien-able right to his own life—proclaimed that his life belonged rather to the state—and spawned virulently altruist-collectivist doctrines that led, inexorably, to totalitarian socialist regimes, first in Russia, then in Italy, and shortly in Germany itself. The history of the twentieth cen-tury featured a desperate struggle to maintain freedom in the Western nations, to preserve it first via a death struggle against Fascism, and then in a forty-five-year "cold war" against Communism.

The menace was German philosophy embodied in sundry Euro-pean totalitarian states. The Islamists, eclipsed by the rise of Europe, dominated now by spectacular Western advance, wallowed in abysmal poverty, licked their wounds, but still nursed an unrelinquished faith-based vision of apocalyptic global conquest. And nobody—*nobody*—in the West remembered or took them seriously.

The perennial danger was forgotten in the sweep of war against temporary but more imminent foes.

But the dormant menace—lurking, skulking now the backstreets of modern history, never retreating back to the Arabian desert that spawned it—reignited in the late twentieth century; erupted first in the Khomeini Revolution in Iran, and subsequently in the triumph of the mujahideen over the Soviets in Afghanistan—aided heavily by the U.S. Government—and by the eventual collapse of the Soviet Union, leaving but one remaining superpower as obstacle in the jihadists' path.

And the West was weary. Dominated for at least a century by the same anti-reason, anti-freedom German doctrines that led to

85

National Socialism and Communism, the continental nations no longer possessed moral courage to defend themselves, and cowered now before the threat of Islam. They signed treaties with Arab nations; bitterly denounced Israel; accepted waves of Muslim immigrants—some of them undeniably jihadists; loudly screamed their tolerance of all creeds—including that of their destroyers—all but that of the Americans, who were "evil imperialists"; placated Islamists at home and abroad for decades; and prepared to live in dhimmitude, as a finally subjugated continent, as, in Bat Ye'or's trenchant term, Eurabia.

Britain and its former North American colony stood alone facing the ancient enemy. And how feeble were their self-crippled efforts. Either unwilling or unable to recognize the terrifying truth confronting him, President Bush believed that the terrorists had "hijacked a great religion." Consequently, he made a "war on terror," not a war on Islamism. The truth is, of course, what it has been for 1,400 years, for Islam's core teachings—based in the perfect word of an eternal book—have remained immutable: *the religion's essence spawns holy warriors against the infidel, terrorists now—not invincible armies—only because the infidel, in the West, has grown too powerful to be currently defeated via all-out war. Jihad has changed forms, is all; its essence is eternally invariant.*

If there be safety now, it is only because the West has grown strong, not because the Islamists have grown peaceable. But, of course, there is no safety. Osama bin Laden's minions drove home that chilling truth; transforming plastic knives, box cutters, and hijacked planes into weapons of mass destruction. In its undiluted evil, Al Qaeda performed Western man a perverse favor, if Western man is only but willing to see; it demonstrated with brutal force the inescapable truth that: *there is no safety against one determined to kill or conquer you, no matter the prospective killer's material weakness. Ideology, not wealth or weapons systems, constitutes the foundation of danger.*

The Islamists cannot currently defeat America—but they can assail and wound it, murder its civilians, cause those living to cower in fear, and, in the absence of overwhelming American military response, nurture a burgeoning dream of America's destruction.

What is, morally and practically, the right step for the United States to now take—and with what intended result?

As in the war against Fascism, so in the current war: the defense of America and American lives requires the utter obliteration of

Islamic Totalitarianism and of its principal engine, representative, and standard bearer—the Iranian regime.

FDR understood this vital point. His words are as true of the war against Islamic Totalitarianism as they were of the war against Fascism. "We have learned that if we do not pull the fangs of the predatory animals of the world, they will multiply and grow in strength...[they] must be disarmed and kept disarmed, and they must abandon the philosophy which has brought so much suffering to the world."

If Americans value their lives and freedom, the Islamists leave open to them but a single course of action to preserve these: a waging of all-out war, both military and philosophic, against religious totalitarianism, beginning with the Islamic Republic of Iran.

Again, the American prosecution of World War II in the Pacific is instructive. The Japanese had conquered the Philippines and much of the South Pacific. They invaded China. They threatened Australia. Recognizing the U.S. Navy's capacity to impede their advance, they savagely bombed Pearl Harbor in attempt to annihilate that obstacle. As a matter of deliberate, cold-blooded policy, they turned loose their troops on conquered civilians to pillage, rape, and murder them by the hundreds of thousands. In the most hideously agonizing fashion, they tortured to death enemy POWs. Their explicit philosophy called for military conquest, a holy duty to vastly expand the Japanese Empire, and need to obliterate all who dared oppose them.

What were America's goals in defending itself from such danger? First and foremost: there would be no negotiated settlement with the Imperial Japanese Government; the Americans would not leave the emperor, his ministers, and their militaristic philosophy in political authority. Unconditional surrender, dismantlement of the regime, and excising of its philosophy were the outcomes recognized as necessary to ensure protection of America and American lives. The first step toward safety lay in inflicting crushing military defeat on Japan.

The Americans turned their overwhelming industrial might to creation of weapons: aircraft carriers, war planes, bombs, etc. They pursued Japanese forces across the Pacific; took island after occupied island; engaged and sank the enemy fleet; blew from the sky his aircraft; and eventually, with history's mightiest navy, surrounded the Japanese Homeland. They showed the enemy no mercy. Historian John Lewis reported that on the night of March 9–10, 1945, U.S. bombers flew at 5,000 feet over Tokyo, "overloaded with incendiary bombs that would be dropped directly on population centers closely packed with balsa wood homes." The result? "A horrendous fire storm aided by 25-knot winds...killed more than 80,000 Japanese." Months later, although Japan was, in fact, devastatingly defeated and lying defenselessly prostrate before American onslaught, its regime still refused surrender. President Truman and his allies were adamant regarding the only acceptable outcome. They stated:

> The full application of our military power, backed by our resolve, will mean the inevitable and complete destruction of the enemy armed forces and just as inevitably the utter devastation of the enemy homeland...
> Following are our terms. We will not deviate from them. There are no alternatives. We shall brook no delay...
> We call upon the enemy to proclaim now the unconditional surrender of all armed forces...The alternative is prompt and utter destruction.

The Japanese regime chose unwisely. It hoped to reach a negotiated settlement with the Americans that would leave in power the emperor, his counselors, and their dreams of world conquest. To achieve this, they readied the nation for an American invasion—to be met by mass suicide attacks by millions of Japanese civilians, as well as by the remainder of its military forces. John Lewis wrote: "All that was needed was for millions of Japanese civilians to be willing to throw their bodies at the Americans in a last charge to protect the Emperor and the Nation." The Americans had not forgotten that victory at Saipan and Okinawa had compelled them to kill almost 98 percent of defending garrisons that, in the face of certain defeat, refused to surrender. "Many in the Japanese military leadership longed for such carnage—as it was their final hope of forcing the Americans to accept Japan's existence as an empire." American military personnel and the nation's commander-in-chief dreaded such a prospect; they estimated an invasion of Japan would result in the death of hundreds of thousands of Americans—and of millions of Japanese civilians; they would have done anything to achieve victory without invasion.

On August 6, 1945, President Truman ordered dropped on Hiroshima an atomic bomb. That day he issued a statement, shortly after dropped as leaflets on Japan, stating that if the enemy regime did not accept American terms, "they may expect a rain of ruin from the air, the like of which has never been seen on this earth." Three days later, as the Japanese regime even more unwisely still refused to surrender, the Americans dropped another, this time on Nagasaki. Finally, on August 10, as thousands of U.S. planes bombed Tokyo and other cities, the Japanese notified the Americans they would accept the victors' terms. They surrendered unconditionally to America.

The devastating military defeat inflicted on Japan was a necessary first step to expunging the threat to America and Americans from Japanese aggression. It was indispensable to shake Japanese thinkers to their philosophic core; to discredit, indeed, disgrace their militaristic ideology; and to cause Japan to radically alter course. This is how a free country "pulls the fangs of the predatory animals of the world." This is the way a war of self-defense against a murderously aggressive foe is properly prosecuted.

This is what today must be done to the Iranian regime.

As a requisite first step of obliterating Islamic Totalitarianism, America must demand of the Iranian Government an immediate unconditional surrender; and, in event of that regime's obdurate recalcitrance, must be willing to deploy the full might of its military—including, if necessary, nuclear weapons—to destroy the country's political leadership, its fanatical mullahs, and its armed forces. As with Germany and Japan in 1945, so Iran today must be mercilessly hammered until and unless its government agrees to America's terms.

In all such cases, full moral responsibility for the deaths of countless innocent civilians lies with the dictators, their supporters and/or terrorist proxies, and the nightmare doctrines that impelled them on a path to world conquest; theories and aggressive practices that necessitated all-out war of self-defense on the part of free nations.

Full military victory today can be achieved much more quickly than America's triumph over Japan—and with minimal loss of American life. John Lewis noted that the United States had no capacity to directly assault Japan in 1941; the Americans necessarily waged naval engagements against the enemy fleet, and bloody infantry battles to re-capture Pacific islands conquered by the Japanese. This took three interminable years of fighting. None of this is required today. "American ingenuity has created an explosion of technology and the possibility of heretofore undreamed of tactics, which make it unnecessary for any American to be killed in the fight. That we have the overwhelming capacity to defeat the Islamic Totalitarians militarily is beyond doubt." Iran, at this war's outset—unlike Germany and Japan in 1941—lies prostrate before America's might; the mullahs have no counter-punch to throw at a withering American strike.

Crushing the Islamist state of Iran accomplishes three major goals: it eradicates the main enemy; it demonstrates American resolve to use all necessary means to gain total victory; and it sends shock waves of terror through jihadists worldwide, who then know they can be next. Briefly, such terror existed after 9/11—but only because of the enemy's fear of what American response could (and should) have been; once America's weak-willed rejoinder became manifest, such terror immediately (and understandably) dissipated.

The only hope of America's enemies—which they know, but we do not—is that America lacks the moral certitude, the will, to wage all-out war against those attacking it. The Islamists state repeatedly, and rely on, the belief that the United States is morally weak, afraid to either inflict or absorb death, and, unlike in World War II, will cut and run at the first sign of massive bloodshed. *The Islamists are right to believe it, because for decades such has been American policy in the Middle East.*

Evidence? President Reagan—Reagan, not Carter—pulled from Lebanon all U.S. forces after Hezbollah's 1983 slaughter of 241 U.S. Marines. No decisive action was ever taken against the lunatic regime of Tehran after its kidnapping of American hostages in 1979. President Clinton pulled from Somalia all U.S. forces after the bloody "Black Hawk Down" battle—an American victory—in 1993.

In addition to running from the enemy, America has often sought to mollify their sensibilities—to repudiate a proper course of action from fear it will enrage and impel them to further aggression. President Bush, for example, accepted Britain and other countries as allies in his "war on terror," but not Israel. His father did the same in the Persian Gulf War of 1990–91, disallowing Israeli participation, even prevailing upon Israel to forego retaliation when Saddam Hussein lobbed missiles into the noncombatant nation. Why not accept military support from an allied nation who fights the same enemy, for the same cause, and does so with great effectiveness? So as not to offend the delicate feelings of the Arab-Islamic world, a culture that, from 1948 to 2011, overwhelmingly refuses to recognize Israel's right to exist, and is dedicated to its utter destruction.

The U.S. government has consistently demonstrated that it is not merely afraid, it is terrified of the Islamists.

A steady procession of U.S. presidents has relentlessly appeased the Islamists in a manner reminiscent of Chamberlain's policy toward Hitler; if none has yet lain supine and begged the enemy's forgiveness for America's existence, such action is, presumably, merely a matter of time. Khomeini was wrong: the "Great Satan" is a laughably inaccurate epithet. The "Great Wimp" is much more truthful. Can any world power, consistently under attack by foes murderous but easily crushed, be more pathetic than America has been for three decades? In comparison to film stars, America is not a "Dirty Harry," Clint Eastwood-style hardass, but a Woody Allen-type nerd. Khomeini and the country's other enemies knew (and continue to know) it. For if America were truly Satanic, i.e., dangerous, her enemies would have long ago suffered the obliteration they so abundantly merit. They yet breathe only by virtue of America's misguided concern for their values, their culture, and their worthless lives.

Perhaps, in some perverse manner, the incessant attacks on America represent a grim form of justice. For if the world's most powerful nation, pre-eminently capable of wreaking its enemy's destruction, refuses to defend itself, it reaps the inevitable harvest of its own milquetoast policies. If a man, regardless of immense power, lies down like a doormat, he cannot wonder that others wipe their feet on him. Nevertheless, many individual Americans, and other victims around the world, are innocent of appeasing the Islamists; it is long past time to bring justice to their murderers, and protection to those still living.

No amount of tough talk unbacked by equally tough deeds will reverse either the reality of American foreign policy or the Islamists' perception of it.

But the utter obliteration of the Iranian regime will.

In one decisive victory, America will then definitively alter thirty years of arrant and pathetic appeasement, and get the terrified attention of jihadists everywhere. It would place the United States squarely on the road to victory, and worldwide, everyone would know it. It would cow our enemies and embolden our allies. Since nothing succeeds like success, it would conjure from the woodwork supporters the nation never knew it had. Innocent human beings in India, in Russia, in Pakistan, in Sudan and other African nations, and across the Arab-Islamic world are understandably terrified of the Islamists; and would tearfully welcome such effacing of danger. Even most Europeans, while safely (and verbally) denouncing "U.S. imperialism," would, in their tiny little hearts, breathe a metaphorical sigh of relief at the excising of the real threat. (Current European attitudes are also perversely understandable; for the Islamists threaten them, and the Americans do not; they are properly unafraid to censure the nonthreat, while quailing piteously before the real one.)

The U.S. Government is frightened, paralyzed with a "deer in the headlights" terror that the "Arab Street" will rise, that the Middle East will be set aflame, and that America will then be immersed in a literal shooting war with not only Islamists but with virtually the globe's entire Muslim population.

Such a conclusion is not merely mistaken; it is irrelevant.

It is mistaken in that it badly miscalculates the purpose and psychology of warfare. Any nation or people that go to war do so in fervent hope of attaining some desired *earthly goal.* No one seeks to die and go to heaven in service of a *hopelessly unachievable ideal.* Because the Islamists are religious zealots who engage in suicide attacks, some people believe they are willing to die for their cause and gain salvation, even if their cause has no possibility of earthly success. This is profoundly false. The Islamists seek not merely salvation in the next life—*but the establishment of theocracy in this one.* For certain, their goals are religious, but, predominantly, they involve the *politicization of religion.* They are holy warriors, fighting for God's Kingdom not merely in Heaven, but on earth. They, like any warriors, hold visions of practical success and are spurred by hopes of ultimate victory. This is why the Islamist movement revived and enormously accelerated *only after* the establishment of the Islamic Republic of Iran. The faithful saw that their earthly dreams were achievable. For as long as they believe it, they will continue to fight, die, and murder Americans.

They will cease and desist only when they are made to realize that their earthly cause is hopeless—and that they, their loved ones, and their children will not merely die—but will die in vain.

They must be made to realize this immediately. A necessary condition of this, an immensely important first step is the inflicting of devastating military defeat on Iran—a U.S. victory that will lend credence to the country's intent to everywhere smash Islamic Totalitarianism, and that will induce all but the most fanatically hardened jihadists to immediately scurry for cover.

What currently enables Islamists to raise converts from the "Arab Street" is their present hope of this worldly victory. The obliteration of such hope will not result in swelling armies of Arab-Islamic jihadists, but in its reverse: the recognition of certain defeat, pessimistic despair, surrender; and, based on these, the possibility of critically re-examining their fundamental philosophy, of doing it publically without fear of murder, and, in time, of changing their minds and their culture.

More important, the above conclusion is irrelevant because America already fights for its life against ideologically driven foes implacably committed to its destruction. The Islamists' philosophy is currently in place, has been since the lifetime of Mohammed, and their present war against America is but continuation of a 1,400-year struggle to impose *sharia* on the globe. American appeasement does not deter, but only fuels such power lust. That they currently possess power merely to harm but not to defeat or destroy us changes this fundamental principle not a whit. They are dangerous due not to their numbers or weapons systems, but to their ideology. Should we wait to defend ourselves until they swell in numbers and/or possess nuclear weapons?

This is philosophic war; given the enemy's intent of world conquest, it is to the death; and the numbers of men fighting on each side is but a secondary issue. Defense of America requires that those fighting for the Islamist ideal must be, regardless their number, offered a single pitiless alternative: unconditional surrender or irrevocable death. The conclusion is stark in its grim simplicity: we must engage and shatter them irrespective of their numbers, for our lives and freedom depend on it.

As a practical point: wars are not won primarily by bodies and their numbers—but by minds and their thinking; not merely regarding strategy, but also by invention and deployment of sophisticated weapons systems. In 1991, for example, American forces in the Persian Gulf did not approximate the million-man army of Saddam Hussein but, nevertheless, employing Cruise missiles, Stealth bombers, and other advanced weapons, won decisive victory. Similarly, in World War II, would the number of fighting men potentially deployed by the Japanese regime have mattered in the face of Harry Truman's decision to drop an atomic bomb?

If a free nation's sole alternative were to appease a small band of implacable killers—or, by vigorous prosecution of defensive war, risk inflaming and greatly expanding the number of assailants, which policy, in the long run, guarantees ongoing murder of its civilians? Refusal to expunge the relentless killers assures continued attacks, some inevitably successful, and endless massacre of civilians. But extirpating such enemies and risking incitement of quiescent sympathizers raises, at minimum and for the first time, the possibility of victory and cessation of assault. When the free nation's overwhelming military might is added to the equation, coupled now for the first time with unwavering resolve to fully deploy it, chance of victory is elevated from possibility to certainty.

After eradicating the regime of the mullahs, America, having demonstrated mettle equivalent to its overpowering might, can proceed to mop up the rest of its enemies. Essentially secular regimes supporting anti-American terrorism, e.g., Bashar Assad's in Syria (and Saddam Hussein's had not Bush foolishly invaded Iraq) could be intimidated into surrender. They would choose the high life of deposed dictators in Paris over certain death for a hopeless cause to which they never subscribed. Hezbollah, bereft of Iranian and Syrian support, would be greatly diminished; withering air strikes against its Lebanese bases would diminish it further.

The Pakistani regime will be told—not asked—that American aircraft, missiles, and bombs will be deployed in that country to whatever degree is necessary to obliterate surviving Al Qaeda and Taliban fighters; the same holds true of Afghanistan or any other country in which jihadists seek sanctuary. The Saudi regime will be ordered to shut down the mosques and madrassahs that preach virulent anti-American hatred; the alternative is that American forces will do so and, at the same time, take back the oilfields developed by Western companies, now to be restored to their proper owners.

While about this, it is necessary to make a clean sweep in the Middle East. American military forces, in conjunction with their Israeli allies, must annihilate Hamas and any other Palestinians overtly dedicated to Israel's destruction. America must lean hard on every Arab-Islamic regime, in every conceivable form, to recognize Israel's right to exist—and to live peaceably with it. The penalty for making war on Israel in any form is to suffer the fate of Iran. With anti-Israel elements expunged from both the Palestinian populace and Arab-Islamic regimes, an independent Palestinian state can then be established—or fifty of them—for none would be dedicated to Israel's destruction. When the dust settles, peace in the Middle East can finally be established, for its foundations would have been laid: the Islamic Totalitarians, like the Fascists of sixty-five years ago, will be dead.

However, total military victory and unconditional surrender of America's enemies is but a necessary pre-condition of enduring success. The United States must wage not merely devastating military war—but all-out philosophic war, as well. America must preach to the entire Arab-Islamic world, in self-confident terms of intellectual–moral certitude, the immense superiority of reason to faith, of secularism to religion, of individualism to tribalism, of freedom to dictatorship, of capitalism to socialism, and of flourishing life to martyrdom in a hopeless cause.

As during the Cold War, when the Voice of America and Radio Free Europe broadcast America's message of liberty and capitalism to the enslaved masses of the Soviet Empire, so it must be today: such messages, in the native tongue of each country, must be ceaselessly beamed, 24/7/365, into every nation of the Arab-Islamic world—if necessary, for centuries. *Atlas Shrugged* must also be translated into every language of the Muslim world—and tens of millions of copies air dropped into each land, a bombardment just as vital to ultimate victory as that of armaments; a bombardment that must continue unabated for decades—again, if necessary, for centuries. Every form of modern media must relentlessly broadcast America's message of reason, secularism, individualism, freedom, and hope: radio, television, the Internet—and books, magazines, pamphlets, and newspapers to be dropped by air.

The unremitting message must be: Political Islam is dead. For the rest of time, it will have no place in governing society. Henceforth, there will be strict legal separation of state and mosque. This campaign will emulate the greatest foreign policy success of American history: the establishment of a free, prosperous society in Japan.

From the late-nineteenth century until its shattering defeat at the hands of the United States, Japanese society was afflicted with a state-imposed religion that demanded worship of its emperor-god. A lengthy quote from John Lewis makes this clear: "The Japanese were motivated by a politicized religious ideology—Shintoism—that posited an all-powerful deity, indoctrinated their children, infected every aspect of their culture, and drove them to suicidal military actions that killed millions." An Imperial order of 1890 "built this 'mytho-religious ideology' into the classroom, making worship of the Emperor and duty to the State into the primary goals of education." Such a fanatical state religion drove Japanese warriors, in the face of certain defeat, to reject surrender in the forms of ritualistic suicide, hopeless "death charges" against overwhelming enemy positions, and kamikaze aerial assaults. State Shinto, much like State Islam, indoctrinated children with worship of death in service of government-backed religion and empire.

95

Following and because of America's decisive victory, the United States was in commanding position to extirpate from Japanese intellectual culture its militaristic philosophy and the established religion upholding it. FDR had said that the world's predatory animals "must abandon the philosophy which has brought so much suffering to the world." The Americans, in accordance with their former commander-in-chief's wisdom, proceeded to enforce precisely such a policy. In October 1945, U.S. Secretary of State, James Byrnes, sent to General Douglas MacArthur, American commander in Japan, a magisterial telegram that stipulated the exact steps to be taken.

> Shintoism, insofar as it is a religion of Individual Japanese, is not to be interfered with. Shintoism, however, insofar as it is directed by the Japanese Government, and as a measure enforced from above by the government, is to be done away with...there will be no place for Shintoism in the schools. Shintoism as a state religion—National Shinto, that is—will go...The dissemination of Japanese militaristic...ideology in any form will be completely suppressed.

America's post-war re-construction of Japan was a victory even more spectacular than its military one. Under American guidance, the Japanese dismantled their militaristic regime, expunged from government their religion of world mastery, exchanged a philosophy of power via conquest for one of prosperity via production, and embarked on a course of unprecedented economic growth. Today, in 2011, Japan is one of the freest, wealthiest, peaceable nations on earth—and a firm ally of its former blood enemy.

Why not the same with Iran?

The parallels regarding the current steps to be taken are striking. John Lewis pointed them out. Paraphrasing the 1945 telegram: "Islam, as it is a religion of individuals, is not to be interfered with. Islam, however, insofar as it is directed by governments, and as a measure enforced from above by any government, is to be done away with." State Islam is to be eradicated. No clerics are to be permitted to serve in government. No government will be officially connected, in any capacity, with any Islamic sect or mosque. Theocracy is to be intellectually refuted, morally discredited, culturally rejected, and politically prohibited. Secularism will rule the state.

It took three-and-a-half years to militarily defeat Japan; twice that to re-construct Japanese society. In the current death struggle, the reverse is true: Iran and other Islamists can be quickly defeated militarily—but full philosophic triumph across the Arab-Islamic world could take centuries.

But before this can happen—as a necessary pre-condition—the Islamists must be made to suffer shattering military defeat. Otherwise, their 1,400-year-old philosophy of religious superiority and rightful world mastery will remain intractably unrevised; for there will exist neither incentive nor opportunity for its widespread challenge. Bernard Lewis wrote: "Usually the lessons of history are most perspicuously and unequivocally taught on the battlefield..." This is accurate neither universally nor necessarily; for rational men need not wage wars—victoriously or otherwise—to be taught revolutionary new truths. But, tragically, it is true for all men who cling to belief—for whichever irrational reason—in rightful world supremacy. They need must have the stuffing beat out of them as a pre-condition of challenging their nightmare doctrines. So it was with both the Germans and the Japanese in the 1940s; so it is with the Islamists today.

When they have been thrashed to a frazzle, when it is unambiguously clear to billions that the Islamist creed led directly to spectacularly thumping defeat —and only at that time—will numerous thinkers rise in the Middle East to challenge that discredited creed; and only then will their physical safety be assured.

It was asserted above that modern philosophy is the principal force holding back America from a righteous war of self-defense. It follows from this that the rejection of such philosophy, and its replacement by theories more rational, is a necessary step toward defeating the Islamists. What specific components of modernism restrict America's application of its military might?

One is the moral rejection of rational egoism for altruism. The rejection of rational self-interest as a proper moral ideal, and its replacement by a code of self-sacrifice, translated into foreign policy means that only wars fought for others, especially the weak, the poor, and/or the non-Western, are virtuous; conflicts waged to advance American self-interest are not. American military intervention in Bosnia, therefore, to rescue the local Muslim population—and serving no discernible American end—was, on this view, morally proper.

On altruist premises, power acquires virtue only when placed in service of those in need. America, as the world's lone superpower, and history's wealthiest nation, is, ipso facto, an imperial aggressor, because the attainment of such haughty stature necessarily involves eschewal of behavior self-denying in favor of that incessantly self-aggrandizing. Only stand-down from such aggression, and surrender of American wealth and values to the world's oppressed, constitutes a path to probity.

John Lewis makes the important point: "In this view, a strong power is good only when it recognizes the moral claims of those in need—even enemies and their supporters. The route to peace is not through victory, since altruism ('otherism') cannot abide the defeat of others." Rather, a better, more peaceful world is reached solely by sharing America's wealth with the impoverished, including with those who seek the country's destruction.

Devastation of the Islamists unambiguously serves America's self-interest; for, by eradicating the latest totalitarian threat, it preserves American lives and freedom. But a great power is not permitted to act in its rational self-interest. It is morally restrained from expunging the jihadists assaulting it; required to fight with merely a fraction of its might; compelled thereby to bog down in unwinnable quagmires; forced to apologize for civilian casualties and/or damage incurred in its war of self-defense; and enjoined to rebuild mosques—sites deemed holy by those seeking America's death—leveled by the fighting.

If America is to survive as a free nation—and if the lives of countless American civilians are to be spared—then the morality of altruism, in all of its hideous facets and iterations, must be unequivocally repudiated for a code properly egoistic. America must understand that just as the good of a rational individual is to pursue his self-interest, so the good of a free society is to do the same; especially when the alternative is to be implacably assaulted by vicious savages impelled by a philosophy straight from the Dark Ages.

But a deeper component of modernist philosophy is also at work—a multi-culturalist, relativist assault on objectivity. To the modernists, following Hume—and Hegel's constructs on a Kantian foundation—there exist no objective moral principles by which to assess the value of any culture; all such principles are social—collectively subjective—arising and applicable solely within a given community or nation; inherently inadequate to judge the value of differing cultures. Americans, therefore, have no cognitive basis to assert the moral superiority of reason to faith, secularism to religion, individualism to tribalism, freedom to dictatorship. Commitment to such principles represents mere cultural bias on the part of Westerners—a prejudice not to be imposed on other cultures.

On this view, it is imperative that we respect the culture of our assailants, learn to understand it, commiserate with the jihadists' frustrated aspirations for world conquest, and bear in mind that our gravest threat is ignorance. Above all, we must not be judgmental.

The Islamists, encumbered with no such drooling subjectivism, claim to hold principles true as universal absolutes; ones not relative to a distinctive culture, and to be imposed authoritatively on all. The problem is not that they lay claim to philosophic absolutes, but to *faith-based, not rationally proven-or-provable ones.* A properly objective moral code is based on the factual requirements of man's life, not on faith-based superstition; necessarily upholds the free-thinking mind—man's survival instrument—and uncompromisingly repudiates any code that subordinates independent rational thought to faith or feelings or any other epistemological candidate.

From Objectivist principles, the current struggle matches America, objectively right but repudiating objectivity, against religious zealots, objectively wrong but embracing (a false view of) objectivity. The American people are, generally, intellectually better; but in terms of each side's leadership, the current struggle, rendered in terms of epistemology, is: cultural relativism versus religion—or subjectivism versus faith—or a mushily "compassionate," timid brand of emotionalism versus a dogmatically, aggressively certain one.

If the philosophy animating our intellectual, moral, and political leadership is not radically altered, we are doomed to defeat, to witness sharia imposed in America, and to be governed by the moral equivalents of Khomeini. Europe is dangerously far along this path, to becoming in Bat Ye'or's trenchant term: "Eurabia." The philosophic explanation is clear: in any death struggle between warring ideologies, one claiming truth and certainty—however irrational its basis—will inevitably "win the hearts and minds" of billions, when the best offered by its foe is skepticism regarding moral absolutes and musty platitudes about admiring the culture of its destroyer.

If the West does not repudiate Modernism for Objectivism, the Islamists will gain the ultimate victory toward which, for 1,400 years, they have relentlessly striven; not by means of military but through philosophic conquest. Westerners will, in time, accept Islam; some from fear, as fanatical foes remorselessly attack men morally uncertain and timidly unwilling to effectually defend themselves; and some from the desperation of intellectual vacuum, which impels them to exchange philosophic nonanswers and moral nonguidance for Islam's rigid certainties.

The philosophic quagmire we have created at home must be escaped as a necessary condition of escaping the military quagmire we have created abroad.

Victory is as possible today as during the 1940s. We do not win today because we do not fight to win. We do not fight to win because we have surrendered the philosophy of victory for the philosophy of appeasement. Victory on the military battlefield requires antecedent victory on the intellectual one. Only when America realizes that its founding philosophic principles are objectively superior to those of its assailants—life-giving as opposed to death-dealing—will it be intellectually and morally empowered to wage decisive war in service of its rational self-interest.

3

A Free Market Solution to Problems of Health Care

Introduction

The U.S. Government is taking the country far down the path leading inevitably to socialized medicine. Nor are these recent developments of the past two or three years; the nation has been on this road for many decades, going back as far as World War II. What are the problems of American medical care—what are their solutions—what are, emphatically, not proper solutions—and why? These questions are of literally life-and-death urgency.

Two important points: (1) The quality of American medical care is excellent. (2) The problem is its cost has become exorbitant, making it impossible for many persons to afford. Evidence for these claims?

First: by almost any rational measure, the quality of U.S. health care is the world's finest. For example: Americans have a higher survival rate than any other country for thirteen of the sixteen most common cancers. *Tens of thousands of international patients travel annually to the U.S. for medical care, including many from Canada's system of socialized medicine—not in the reverse direction.* Fewer than one in five American men with prostate cancer die from it—but 57 percent of English men and nearly half of French and German men do. *If death by motor vehicle accident is subtracted, the American life expectancy is the world's highest.* By 2005, eighteen of the past twenty-five Nobel Prize winners for Medicine were either American citizens or chose to work here. Half of the major new medicines introduced worldwide were developed by American companies. American researchers played a key role in 80 percent of the most important medical advances of the prior thirty years. Dr. Maurice Hilleman and his team at Merck, for example, developed eight of the fourteen vaccines routinely recommended, including for mumps, measles, chicken pox, pandemic flu, hepatitis B, and others. *Hilleman is credited with saving more lives than any other scientist of the twentieth century.*

Given the poor diet of many Americans, and a widespread problem of obesity in the United States, the country's high life expectancy is, in part, a tribute to the quality of its medical care.

Second: regarding rising cost, examples sadly abound. An extended hospital stay can be financially ruinous. The cost of a bed alone, independent of doctor fees, is over $1,000.00 per day, sometimes as much as $1,500.00. A simple Tylenol tablet often costs $20.00. Measured in constant dollars, annual medical spending in the United States exploded over the course of the twentieth century, rising from $155.00 per capita in 1919 to almost $4,000.00 in recent years. The U.S. Government figures report that physician services quadrupled in price between 1946 and century's end—and continue to rise. Nobel Prize–winning economist, Milton Friedman, wrote that: "Expressed as a fraction of national income, spending on medical care went from 3 percent of the national income in 1919 to 4.5 percent in 1946, to 7 percent in 1965, to a mind-boggling 17 percent (highest in the world by far) in 1997"—and then continued to rise.

The result is that uninsured individuals live as much in dread of hospitalization's cost as they do of serious illness itself. Unfortunately, there are many in this predicament, for today tens of millions of Americans are uninsured.

What is responsible for such insanity? And what is the solution?

Because the problem of American medical care is not its quality but its expense, the exact question becomes: how to retain the quality of care while dramatically diminishing its cost? This problem can be resolved. In logic, the first step is to identify the specific causes of the cost's astronomical rise, then the proper means to roll it back.

At the outset of our investigation, it must be made clear that America is no longer a capitalist system, and has not been so for at least as far back as FDR's New Deal in the 1930s. America is, and has been for many decades, a thoroughly mixed economy, a farrago of clashing elements—part capitalist, part socialist; part freedom, part statism; part private ownership, part government controls. One way of formulating the fundamental questions is to examine them from this perspective. Which part of the mixture leads to medical care's high quality? Which part leads to its high cost? Which part of the mixture is life-advancing and to be preserved? Which part is life-threatening and to be excised? Answers to such questions provide indispensable knowledge enabling Americans to rectify the country's health care problems.

The price of any product or service—call it X—rises when demand exceeds supply, and rises enormously when demand enormously exceeds supply. Therefore, some factor(s) have either caused demand for medical services to rise, or supply of them to decline, or both. What is the truth? Start first with increasing demand—and look at the history.

The Causes of Rising Medical Costs

Government-mandated wage and price controls during World War II prevented employers from offering higher wages as a means of attracting workers. With workers in short supply due to the war, employers began offering health insurance benefits as a means of gaining the most qualified employees. The government did not regard this as a wage increase and consequently did not tax it. After the war, labor unions avidly sought such perks for their members; backed by the coercive power of the state, legally requiring employers to negotiate with them, unions imposed it as a routine feature of contract demands. The result was that by 1960 employer-provided health insurance was deeply entrenched in the U.S. economy.

The government continued to encourage this method by treating medical benefits as distinct from income, and refusing to tax it. But if an employee received in cash the equivalent of his employer's expense on his health care policy—and then used it to purchase his own policy—he would pay taxes on the additional income. The government's tax policy thereby made it seem attractive to gain third-party, employer-provided coverage. This point is important—and will be returned to.

By the 1960s, millions of American families were no longer paying out-of-pocket for most of their medical costs.

Related: in 1965, Congress—driven by the same altruist-collectivist premises that actuate all socialist policies—passed legislation establishing the Medicare and Medicaid programs, to pay the medical care of the elderly and poor, respectively. Medicare and Medicaid, in conjunction with employer-provided health coverage, meant that a third-party payment system now dominated the American medical field.

Medical care had, in effect, become socialized. Most Americans now had to pay nothing (or at most a modest deductible and even more modest co-payment) for treatment. Medical care for tens—if not hundreds—of millions was now virtually free.

What will it do to the demand for X when its price drastically falls? Put simply: no individual, no matter his scrupulous honesty, spends the money of some established institution—whether government, employer, or insurance company—as frugally as he does his own. *Where powerful institutions provide powerful financial incentives in support of paternalistic care in any field, the inevitable result is an undermining of personal responsibility regarding that field.*

Nobel Laureate Milton Friedman provides a more technical answer: "the lower the price, the greater the quantity demanded; at a zero price, the quantity demanded becomes infinite." In any terms, demand for X skyrockets.

Examine this point by process of analogy. Food is substantially more important to human life and well-being than is medical care. Millions of persons might go years without need of medical care, but they require food on a daily basis, and perish in roughly three weeks in its absence. Suppose tens of millions of employees ate due to employer-provided food coverage. Suppose the government, in its compassion for the needy, determined to ensure the availability of plentiful food for all, and established Foodcare and Foodaid to provide it for the elderly and the indigent. What will be the inevitable consequences?

Since individuals now pay a pittance for food, if anything, they might as well dine sumptuously. They can now afford the highest quality and the greatest quantity; they can gorge, hoard, waste, and feed filet mignon to the cat. Where previously, budgetary constraints limited many people to procuring food at the local supermarket, now they can patronize five star restaurants and high-end gourmet establishments.

Farmers, restaurateurs, and supermarket owners are, of course, ecstatic. Demand for food has soared, people want the best—and price is no object. Since customers do not themselves pay for food, they have no incentive to care about its price. If customers have no reason to be concerned with prices, then producers need not worry about competitors' underselling them, and can charge any price they want. Why not? Employers and/or insurance companies and/or the government will pick up the tab.

The lesson is clear: there is no limit to demand if those who purchase or consume a product do not themselves pay for it. As one essayist wrote: "Prices will skyrocket if there's no limit to how much people can spend on a product. If anyone who wants a product can buy it, price no object, there is absolutely no reason for the manufacturer to try to cut his prices, and no reason for the buyer to control how much he spends."

As with food, there is no limit to demand for medical care. For example, countless millions of individuals each year suffer from colds, sore throats, upset stomachs, scrapes, bruises, and minor aches and pains, the overwhelming bulk of which are self-healing ailments. In many such cases, individuals neither need nor seek medical attention. But not all are so hardy in outlook, and, if the price is right, prefer to see a doctor. Often, if medical care is "free," they will seek it; if it is not, they will permit the malady to heal itself.

Further, tens of millions suffer from various chronic ailments—insomnia, allergies, bad backs, etc. For many suffering such ongoing discomfort, treatment seems a viable option, despite gaining limited or no relief from it. Again, if they need not pay, they often seek medical intervention.

One striking example was provided by a letter from a physician to the *New York Times*. He had, he said, an eighty-year-old patient who suffered from the condition of "slowing down." Though informed that such a condition was not unusual, the patient and his family chose to embark on a Medicare shopping spree. The patient proceeded to undergo a CAT scan, an MRI examination, a spinal tap, a brain stem evoke potential, and a carotid duplex ultrasound. The tests revealed no remediable problems and cost in excess of $4,000.00. The physician said he had seen other cases of such third-party-payer madness.

Notice that, in the numbers provided above from Milton Friedman, *the enormous rise in medical cost is a post-1960s development.* Prior to this, doctors made house calls (which the author is old enough to remember), their fees were affordable by the overwhelming bulk of the population, and a hospital stay was worrisome exclusively for medical—not financial—reasons. The contrast between pre-and-post-1960s medical cost can be stated starkly: the patient paid less than $10.00 for a doctor to visit him—or he currently pays in excess of $100.00 to visit a doctor.

Why do doctors no longer make house calls? Because their services are in a demand too high for them to spend time in transit. Why has the cost of medical care jumped astronomically? Because the third-party-payer system astronomically supercharged demand by relieving individual patients of the responsibility to pay their own medical expenses. Evidence? By the turn of the twenty-first century, only five cents of every dollar of hospital income, and only nineteen cents of each dollar of physician fees, were paid by patients spending their own money. By that time, fewer than 15 percent of Americans were responsible for paying their own medical fees. For the rest, health care was provided by a third party.

Further, in addition to immensely expanding demand, the government's actions have also severely restricted the supply of medical care. It has done this by establishing state licensing boards for physicians and allowing the American Medical Association (AMA) to control these regulatory bodies. For decades, the AMA has restricted entry into the field of medicine by means of medical licensing laws.

The AMA, formed in 1847, committed itself immediately to elevating the educational standards of U.S. medical schools, thereby providing students with an outstanding education, and ensuring high quality of medical care. Unfortunately, the AMA sought to implement such goals by means of government controls. By the early twentieth century, all state legislatures had established Boards of Medical Examiners, generally staffed by AMA members, to license aspiring physicians and to set medical school standards.

The AMA has long feared that the United States suffered from a glut of doctors, and has striven to reduce the supply. The organization recommended that a large number of medical schools be closed, that standards be raised in the rest, and that admission be sharply restricted. With the power of state governments behind it, the AMA succeeded in reducing the number of U.S. medical schools from 162 in 1910 to 85 in 1920—to 76 in 1930—and to 69 in 1944. (They particularly targeted those schools specializing in the training of black physicians; between 1910 and 1944, for example, the number of black medical schools fell from seven to two.

The AMA's stated goal was to protect the public by ensuring a high quality of medical care—and to do so by having fewer doctors who were more highly trained. In effect, individuals would be protected against lesser but still competent doctors by legislating out of existence medical schools lesser but still competent. One analyst wryly noted regarding such a policy that it was as if all would have Cadillacs if state governments would but outlaw Fords.

The inevitable (and intended) result has been a diminished supply of physicians, reduced competition, rising prices, and increased income for doctors. The AMA's policy of restricting entry into the medical field has debarred many effective (if not outstanding) physicians—and has necessarily raised both medical prices and doctors' incomes.

Milton Friedman provides a striking example of this point. In the 1930s, many highly trained, experienced German and Austrian physicians flowed into the United States, fleeing National Socialism—but the number of foreign-trained doctors admitted into American medical practice in the five years after Hitler's ascent to power was no greater than during the five years preceding it. That such European practitioners were as highly skilled as their American counterparts, there is no doubt. Restricting them from the field did not increase medical standards; it merely reduced competition.

Reduction of supply of X relative to demand for it, necessarily increases prices.

The members of virtually every profession have, at one time or another, clamored for government licensing requirements in the name of protecting the public. Several have succeeded, including dentists, lawyers, cosmetologists, plumbers, and morticians, whose members compose the state licensing boards and proceed to restrict entry to the respective fields. According to the Federal Trade Commission (FTC), there exists an endless procession of occupational groups lobbying legislatures in the hope of establishing state certification boards controlled by their members; a procession including well diggers, home improvement contractors, appraisers, TV repairmen, as well as others.

The key to understanding the phenomenon of legally restricted entry is to observe that *it is not consumers lobbying state legislatures for such "protection"; it is the members of the profession.* Regrettably, some producers seek to increase market share by legally restricting the number of competitors who can enter their field.

Finally, as noted above, food is even more urgent in human life than is medical care—and it can spoil, and/or be poorly prepared, and/or be ill protected from pests by growers. People can be made sick through food poisoning, and perhaps even die. To obviate such concerns, and protect the public, surely the government should establish state certification boards, staffed by expert farmers, chefs, bakers, butchers, and restaurateurs, to license candidates to grow, prepare, and serve food. Since the possibility of accident, serious injury, and/or death is inherent in every moment and activity of human life, the exact argument, on identical grounds, can be made regarding automotive repair men, architects, construction workers, taxi drivers, highway maintenance crews, nannies, babysitters, and a host of other professions. It is eminently debatable that such government licensing boards staffed by professional experts would "protect the public"; for the resulting shortage of producers might make a vital good or service unavailable to (or unaffordable by) sundry individuals, much to the impoverishment, perhaps even endangerment of their lives. There is a vastly better way to protect the rights and lives of patients/customers, as will be seen shortly.

By actions that both stimulate demand for medical services and limit its supply, the government has inevitably raised medical prices. There is no more escape from the laws of economics than there is from the laws of physics; for if demand for X is dramatically invigorated, while its supply is simultaneously suppressed, steeply increasing prices is as inescapable as a hard plummet to earth for one who steps off the observation deck of a popular urban skyscraper. In short, the results of such governmental actions in the medical marketplace were eminently predictable.

The problem with contemporary American medical care, in brief, is third-party payment. The cause, stated even more briefly, is: government. In summary: the federal government, via Medicare and Medicaid, has, in effect, socialized health care for the elderly and poor; and, by means of tax incentives—and legislation empowering coercive unions—is responsible for employer-provided, third-party insurance payments for much of the remaining population.

What is the solution to the nightmare created by government intervention in the health care market? It is clear how America got into the current fiasco. How does it now get out? What are the practical steps? Above all, what are the relevant moral principles?

Resolving the Problem

In broad terms, the solution is simple: get the government the hell out of the medical field and establish a free market of medicine. For example, regarding food, America has something much more closely resembling a free market than it has regarding medical care. In the overwhelming number of cases, individuals are responsible for their own food expenses. The result is that demand is not enormously increased relative to supply, prices remain relatively stable and low, and an immense majority of Americans can afford adequate quantities of nutritious food. Observe that nobody clamors for government reform of the food industry or for a move toward "socialized agriculture."

(A basically good situation can be made even better. Government does stimulate demand by issuing food stamps. Similarly, it does suppress supply by paying U.S. farmers not to grow food. By expunging both policies, the government would get out of the food industry, re-establish a free market in the field, increase supply of foodstuffs relative to demand for them, and consequently lower food prices.)

Medicine, unlike agriculture, has already been socialized to a significant degree. What practical steps are necessary to effectively roll back the socialization and, once again, properly restore a free market in the field?

As a pre-condition of answering the practical question, the current state of health insurance can and must be contrasted with other important forms of insurance. Health insurance in contemporary America has morphed into something unrecognizable in comparison to auto or home insurance. For example, an insurance company does not pay for everyday maintenance on an individual's car or home. If a man hires a mechanic to repair the brakes on his car—or a roofer to re-shingle his home—he typically pays the bills out of his own pocket. The insurance policy generally provides coverage only for catastrophic occurrences, e.g., the car is severely damaged in an accident or his house catches on fire. Both the premiums for such policies and the out-of-pocket expenses incurred are affordable by the overwhelming majority of Americans. People generally do not want to use their insurance; it is purchased as protection against unexpected, catastrophic events. Consequently, the cost of auto or home repair is affordable; prices have not risen to the insane heights seen in the medical field.

But what would happen to the price of auto repair if everyday maintenance were funded by some combination of government and employer-provided insurance? Brake replacement, body work, new tires, tune ups, oil changes, engine overhaul, etc., are then virtually free of charge. The same economic principles apply, the same consequences ensue, and, once again, we see demand enormously increased, and prices rise to heights unaffordable for those uninsured.

In light of this, to cure the health care crisis it is essential to eliminate all government legislation, programs, and tax incentives designed to eradicate personal responsibility and establish third-party medical payments. The means to do this are straightforward and are not rocket science to understand. What is necessary are practical steps that will simultaneously diminish demand and increase supply. Such steps will bring medical prices down to a level affordable by an overwhelming majority of Americans. It will put responsibility for medical payment back where it belongs—in the hands of the patients, who will then be free to choose their own doctors, their own insurance coverage, their own treatment, and its date.

The first necessary step is to decrease the enormous current demand for medical care, which can be accomplished by a simple change in the tax code. Employers must be free to offer their employees a choice between continued employer-provided health insurance, on the one hand, and tax-free income in an amount equivalent to the policy's cost, on the other. (Early in the new millennium, this cost was generally around $5,000.00.) Employees would then realize that they are responsible for their own medical payments; for even if they opted to remain under present coverage, they would realize that it was potentially costing them thousands of dollars of annual tax-free income.

The advantage to this is that it provides financial incentive for employees to purchase an insurance policy with both a high deductible and extensive coverage for hospitalization and/or major medical problems. If the deductible is as high as two or three thousand dollars per year, it will discourage doctor visits for minor, self-healing ailments. It will eliminate the problem of hypochondriacs and malingerers clogging doctors' waiting rooms. Once individuals pay out of their own pockets for ordinary, everyday medical care, demand for such will be significantly reduced.

The price for such a policy is roughly one-half the average paid by employers for each employee, and is easily affordable by a worker now making an additional $5,000.00 of tax-free annual income. Further, an employee now has the money to pay the deductible, if necessary—and, since he retains whatever is unspent on medical bills, he possesses financial incentive to keep medical expenses down. Under this approach, most Americans will have used less medical care and will possess increased savings at year's end.

It makes economic sense that health insurance be treated in the same way as other important forms of insurance. Individuals should pay all routine medical expenses out of their own pockets—and, additionally, purchase their own insurance with both a high deductible and extensive catastrophic coverage. Such a policy is cheaper than the employer-provided policies held currently by many persons, and provides the only coverage that is generally personally unaffordable: payment for lengthy hospital stays and/or significant medical treatment. Best of all, it takes control of large numbers of medical decisions out of the hands of third-party payers, placing it back in the hands of the patients in concert with their doctors.

No third party either pays for or controls an individual's decisions regarding the consumption of life's even more urgent necessity—food—and, similarly, none should do so regarding medical care.

A current option that should be expanded is the establishment of medical savings accounts (MSAs). As one writer regarding affordable medical care states: "An MSA is an individual savings account to pay uninsured medical expenses, which is coupled with a catastrophic health insurance policy." MSAs could be set up either by individuals or groups—or by employers for their workers.

An individual, in establishing an MSA, could choose to use tax-free income in an amount equivalent to what his employer previously paid for his health insurance. Each year, he could deposit some amount of his income in the MSA to help pay for his (and his family's) medical costs. Since it is his money, it would be portable if he changed jobs. Because he retains what is not spent, he is motivated to keep down medical expenditures.

With an MSA, customers have no restrictions. They choose their own doctors and specialists; they are free to seek discounts and negotiate costs; above all, they "control the medical decisions with their doctor's advice, without third party intervention...There is no more powerful economic force than a consumer empowered with his own money."

Employees benefit under this type of plan; for insurance policies with a high deductible come with a low premium. In any given year, roughly 70 percent of people have very few medical expenses—and, with financial incentives, could be motivated to lower such expenses still further; as a result, they will save money with this type of insurance policy.

Economic studies show that, in general, the amount of medical care people consume varies with the out-of-pocket price they pay. For example, a Rand Corporation study identified several important facts: people who received free care spent approximately 50 percent more than those who paid 95 percent of medical costs out of their own pockets (on policies with deductibles up to $1,000.00.) "People who had free care were about 25 percent more likely to see a physician and 33 percent more likely to enter a hospital." Significantly, despite these differences in consumption of medical care, the study found no difference in the general health of members of the two groups.

The overall lesson is: although it is far easier to spend other people's money, the results in medical care are vastly higher prices, not superior health.

Actions must also be taken to diminish Medicare and Medicaid spending. Ultimately, both Medicare and Medicaid—and the entire welfare system—should be phased out entirely. But America can begin with several reform measures. First, at the age of sixty-five, every individual should be given the opportunity to sign away his legal rights to Medicare and Social Security in exchange for tax-exempt status for the rest of his life on all income from any source whatever—wages, salaries, or self-employment. Additionally, the money he makes from interest or dividends on this tax-free income should also be tax-exempt. Finally, whatever wealth he bestows on his heirs from such untaxed income should be exempt from inheritance and gift taxes. Such policies provide a powerful set of financial incentives for elderly individuals to opt out of the Medicare and Social Security programs.

This would transform the years of former retirement into the period of the greatest financial freedom of an individual's lifetime.

In addition, the law should be amended so that individuals approaching retirement age would know in advance that in a specified number of years—five, for example—retirees would be required to pay a deductible of two or three thousand dollars before their Medicare coverage begins. They should also pay more than a minimal co-payment for medical services. The requirement of personal financial responsibility will decrease demand for medical care, while the five-year grace period will enable people approaching retirement to save money and prepare for the new circumstances.

Presumably, the huge financial benefits offered for opting out of the Medicare and Social Security systems, and continuing to work, will motivate many persons to do exactly that. Those in financial need will rely on the voluntary charity of doctors and private donors, which was both a common and effective means by which the elderly and/or needy received medical care in the days prior to Medicare and Medicaid.

Bear in mind that private Americans donate several hundreds of billions of dollars to charity annually; that Habitat for Humanity, one such voluntary organization, builds homes for poor persons; and that Doctors Without Borders provides free medical care to needy individuals worldwide. There is dearth of neither wealth nor generous donors in America, and every expectation that the dismantling of the welfare state will coincide with the establishment of private charities to assist the elderly and needy with medical expenses.

In addition to reducing demand for medical care, practical steps can be taken to increase its supply. For example, regarding the doctors' legitimate concern for patient safety, the free market is best equipped to handle it. First, under a system of individual rights, nobody could claim education or training they did not possess. This is fraud, and is properly punishable by the criminal justice system.

Related, in a free country nothing prevents physicians from outstanding medical schools forming private organizations to observe and certify every medical practitioner in the country. Such organizations could include the exact physicians currently staffing the state certification boards. They could even publish a *Medical Consumer Reports* to publicize their findings, thereby providing an immensely important service, and probably earning from it a well-deserved profit. If a physician could advertise on his shingle, in the Yellow Pages, on-line, or anywhere else that he received "the AMA's highest rating," it would be a great boon to his practice; medical practitioners would compete for such an endorsement; and, if some medical provider refused to be observed and included in the AMA's report, that decision, too, would provide information to a responsible consumer.

But under such a system, the doctors would lack the legal authority to coercively enforce their standards. They could neither forcibly restrict noncertified practitioners from entering the field nor prevent patients from patronizing them for treatment. Each patient for himself, and parents for their children—not the state—would decide the merit of a medical provider; similarly, regarding the worth of the assessment offered by private medical examining organizations. If patients respect the work of their health care provider, the state could not coercively prevent them from employing his services.

Freedom means choice, liberals like to say specifically regarding abortion. The principle is true, and applicable to wider issues, including that of health care.

An ongoing example of this principle is that of chiropractors, who provide treatment for pain (often of the back and lower body) by means of manipulation (as of the spinal column). Despite the AMA's long opposition to chiropractic, patients often report that chiropractors afford them more relief from back pain than do physicians. If the AMA ever succeeded in legally banning this practice, patients would no longer be free to exercise their own judgment regarding such maladies.

113

There also exist highly knowledgeable individuals among the ranks of paramedics, registered nurses, and licensed pharmacists, who, in numerous cases, are capable of providing competent medical care. As but one example, Milton Friedman points out that after the introduction of paramedics to the medical field, the survival rate of patients whose hearts stopped during cardiac arrest rose dramatically. If an individual—despite absence of training from an AMA-approved medical school—can help save a heart attack victim, is it not possible that he might assist those suffering from head colds, sore throats, or upset stomachs?

Further, on a free medical marketplace, where physicians can neither debar entry to such competent competitors, nor restrict patients patronizing them, it would be in the self-interest of all for doctors to train and absorb into their practices as "associate physicians" the best of such practitioners. It is in the self-interest of the physician because he can broaden his practice by subordinating a qualified competitor under his auspices; in the self-interest of the "associate" because he now acquires training and the respectability of junior partnership with an AMA-approved physician; and in the self-interest of patients because there are now more qualified doctors competing for business, with a consequent diminishing of medical prices. Who knows? Perhaps increased competition will even motivate such "associate physicians" to (once again) make house calls regarding routine ailments and childhood illnesses, reviving that ancient, honorable practice and all the convenience attached to it.

Finally, an important political point: under the current government-controlled medical marketplace, the members of medical licensing boards are appointed by state governors and legislators. These lawmakers are elected by the voters. If voters have sufficient capacity to select those who control medical decisions—not to mention national officeholders who decide vastly more complex issues of domestic and foreign policy—then, in principle, they certainly possess capacity to directly choose their own physicians. In logic, if they lacked ability to wisely select their doctors, they would necessarily lack ability to wisely select politicians who, in effect, appoint their doctors.

Why is a free market of medicine immensely superior to statist medicine? Of all the complex factors making up the answer, the most important is: freedom protects the right of each individual to live in accordance with his own best judgment.

In practice, this means that those who love medicine are free to pursue it as a career. Entrepreneurs who love research are free to found pharmaceutical or biotech companies, and those who regard them as potentially profitable to invest their funds. Physicians are free to compete for customers; patients are free to choose their own medical provider; and those doctors sincerely concerned with patient safety are free to establish private medical certification boards and publish their findings.

Earlier was discussed the staggering intellectual advances made possible under the system of individual rights. Such pioneering accomplishments emphatically include the field of medicine. From Walter Reed's breakthrough regarding yellow fever to Jonas Salk's vaccine for polio—from Maurice Hilleman's revolutionary work in vaccinology to the mass production of penicillin—from open heart surgery to the creation of MRI machines—from great progress in dentistry to treatments for depression and other psychological ailments—to immensely more—the health care advances of the capitalist era dwarf those of preceding centuries. Such breakthroughs demonstrate in a new form the same principle: when man's right to his own mind is protected—when individuals are free, not subordinate to the state—innovative thinkers revolutionize every intellectual field.

Why, under a free market of medicine, did it cost under ten dollars for a doctor's house call and less than one hundred dollars for a night in a hospital? Because the government was not granted power to immensely stimulate demand for medical services by establishing, in multiple forms, a third-party-payer system. Patients, employing their own money and thinking, and in concert with the knowledge and recommendations of their physicians—not the government or insurance companies—chose the medical treatments appropriate to them.

The questions were raised at the chapter's outset: which part of America's current mixed economy is responsible for the high quality of American medical care—and which part responsible for its high cost? These questions have been answered. The freer, capitalist element is responsible for America's outstanding medical care; the government-controlled, socialist element for its exorbitant cost.

The political impetus of the past sixty years in medicine, including the establishment of Obamacare, is toward increasing governmental control of the medical field; indeed, toward socialized medicine. The horrors of such a system are manifest.

In such countries as England, Sweden, Germany, and Canada, the government provides all medical care; in England, since 1948. It is generally free (except for the exorbitant tax rates necessary to finance it) and popular with the voters. But how effective is its care, especially for the seriously ill? Judging by the evidence, medical care is often poor.

Overutilization caused by zero price leads to lengthy waiting lists for many services. Further, since excessive demand causes rising costs and budgetary constraints, a socialist regime possesses diminished funds to allocate toward physicians. Because less money is spent on doctors, there is less to spend on medical training. Socialist governments necessarily train more general practitioners and fewer specialists, whose education involves a greater investment of time and money.

The German Government, for example, restricts the amount of openings allocated for training specialists. As one consequence, the country has few neurosurgeons. An American neurosurgeon examined patients ("victims" one writer on health care termed them) whose head injuries and ailments were operated on by general surgeons, and reported that whereas such patients in America would have been restored to functioning health, German medical care left them as "gorks," i.e., as patients suffering severe and irreversible brain damage.

Similarly, Canada has 11 heart surgery facilities (one for every 2.3 million residents) compared to the United States, which has 793 (one for every 300,000 residents). It need not be wondered which country provides a greater preponderance of heart specialists. One result is waiting lists for persons who critically need cardiac care. Cardiac surgeons report patients dying while on their waiting lists. During the 1990s, Heartbeat Windsor, a private charity organization, helped Canadians obtain critically needed surgery in the United States. In Ontario alone, more than six hundred critically ill patients were sent for care to the United States between the 2003–04 fiscal year and 2008; other provinces report the same sad phenomenon. In 2007, Canadians requiring surgery waited for more than eighteen weeks.

These are inevitable results of increasing demand for medical services and diminishing the supply of qualified practitioners; consequently, they are endemic in nations suffering under the yoke of socialized medicine. In Sweden, for example, a government commission on coronary care found that Swedes can wait up to eleven months for a diagnostic heart X-ray, and up to eight months for essential heart surgery. A cardiologist researching such problems calculated that one thousand Swedes annually, needlessly die for lack of adequate cardiac treatment.

In England, men over age sixty-five generally cannot receive kidney dialysis. In 2009, the National Health Service, trying to control costs, banned three of four new treatments for kidney cancer, adopting a one-size-fits-all policy to the immense disadvantage of the seven thousand patients diagnosed each year with the ailment. The countless patients who prematurely die because of shortages and waiting lists due to socialized medicine are too many to accurately estimate.

Since extended waiting periods exist even for life-and-death cases, it stands to reason that for elective surgeries the wait is even longer. In England, for example, by the turn of the millennium, more than one million patients were on the waiting lists for elective surgery, and the government acknowledged that at least 25 percent of them would be kept waiting for more than a year. In 2009, 230,000 Britons were forced to wait more than 18 weeks for hospital treatment. An English orthopedic surgeon stated that an elderly patient awaiting hip replacement would likely die before reaching the top of the list. Dr. John Cozens-Hardy, one of the nation's top orthopedic specialists, believed his prospective patients had a right to know why they spent years "imprisoned by pain." He told them that at present rates it would take thirty-six years to clear the people on his waiting list. The interminable wait was a result of ongoing shortage of hospital beds, operating rooms, and competent staff. The waiting lists to enter English and German hospitals are so long that patients, long recovered, often forget the reasons they originally applied for admission.

But it is free.

Or is it? In two important ways, it is not. The obvious one is the exorbitant tax rates required to fund it. When citizens are robbed of vast quantities of their earnings, it limits the amount of money they can save, or spend on food, clothing, housing, or education for themselves or their children. It depletes the amount of capital available to found entrepreneurial ventures or to invest in them. It undermines the activities they can undertake either during their working years or in retirement. It diminishes the funds available to spend on recreation, entertainment, and vacation. In countless ways, the confiscatory tax system reduces the amount of fulfillment possible to mankind's best members: the hard-working, productive men and women who finance all coercive governmental programs.

117

In addition to the unconscionable tax rates for "free" medical care, patients pay in a second form: by means of the hours spent waiting in doctors' offices and emergency rooms. The busy professional man or woman has far more productive things to do than spend hours idling in a waiting room. "Time is money," the saying truthfully goes, and time subtracted from productive activities means that much less wealth created by men.

For millions of healthy persons, who might go years without visiting a doctor, the irretrievably lost income that might have been deployed in service of myriad values, brings them no offsetting benefit. Further, millions of elderly or seriously ill persons who, for years, paid the crippling taxes that finance the system, were robbed for naught; in their hour of gravest need, the system effectually abandons them to debilitating pain and/or premature death.

An important, oft overlooked point: because free-on-demand medical care is so expensive, governments that provide it possess severely diminished funds to allocate toward medical research. Heavily taxed private citizens have less disposable income to invest in private, profit-driven pharmaceutical or biotech companies. Consequently, most new medications, pioneering treatments, and revolutionary surgical procedures originate in the countries that support greater freedom in the medical field, i.e., in the United States. Since men create values primarily by thinking, political–economic freedom is essentially freedom of the mind. What happens to medical research when free markets have been expunged and replaced by socialized systems? What follows when free minds are increasingly subordinate to budgetary restrictions and governmental edict? What occurs when the United States excises all capitalist elements from its superlative medical field? The answer is obvious: a diminishment of advance in medical research.

What is the final verdict regarding socialized medicine? It provides satisfactory health care for those maladies treatable by general practitioners, albeit with extensive wait time—maladies that are often self-healing; it is poor regarding critical, urgent, and/or life-and-death care; and the punishing tax code sustaining it robs men of wealth they could otherwise employ to immensely improve their lives. In short, productive men are fleeced of huge portions of their earnings in return for painfully little. Such an exchange provides abysmally poor value for patients, especially when contrasted with the care possible under a free market of medicine.

Why then do large portions of the globe tolerate socialized medicine—and why does the United States totter toward it?

Economically, socialism, in all of its hideous iterations, is an abysmal failure. It is propped up solely by moral–political arguments—by the claim that a man is his brother's keeper and that, therefore, a proper government must coercively enforce each individual's unchosen moral obligations to others. Such an altruist moral code has been dominant in Western society for at least as long as has been Christianity; its political application became ascendant due to the influence of modern socialist intellectuals, of whom Karl Marx is one prominent example. This belief, applied to health care, means that medical care is a right of all, without regard to what an individual earns or can pay for.

Such a claim represents a profound moral error.

A right involves an individual's freedom to pursue the values his life requires. Since an individual's survival necessitates he gain food, clothing, shelter, etc., it is morally incumbent that he be left free to take all actions requisite to acquiring them. But rights involve freedom of action; not guaranteed access to somebody else's property. They entail liberty to take the practical steps necessary to create the values required by life. In brief, a man has the right to what he works for and earns.

The socialist claim that a man has a right to some commodity—whether food, medical care, or another—regardless whether or not he has earned it, obliterates all legitimate rights. For if he does not earn it, at whose expense does he gain it? Obviously, other people's. His right to unearned food or health care imposes obligations to supply such goods on those who have created them. The government, of course, levies taxes to enforce such unchosen obligations, and productive persons are then forced to support those unproductive. What has become of their rights? What has happened to their freedom? They have lost their inalienable right to pursue their own values, their own success, their own happiness. They exist now in involuntary servitude to the needy.

There can be no such thing as a right that obliterates the rights of others.

Philosopher, Leonard Peikoff, wrote: "Observe that all legitimate rights have one thing in common: they are rights to actions, not to rewards from other people." Since a man can be prevented from pursuing his interests solely by the initiation of force against him, it follows that his basic right is to freedom of action. Society, i.e., all other

119

men, must respect an individual's right to work for those values necessary to sustain his life. To that end, society must be legally constrained from coercively interfering with an individual's pursuit of values. This, and nothing else, is what it means to have rights. Absent this, there is no such thing as liberty. Peikoff wrote: "Your right to happiness at [other's] expense means that they become rightless serfs, i.e., your slaves. Your right to anything at other's expense means that they become rightless."

A man has the right to all those things he earns by his own effort and/or through free trade, with the voluntary consent of those with whom he trades. He has no right to what belongs to others except as they voluntarily agree to provide it. This applies to medical care as much as to anything else. An individual has the right to health care if he can pay for it, i.e., if he earns it by means of his own productive work. In this regard, it is no different than food, clothing, or shelter—values even more vital for man's survival—and which Americans provide for themselves, free of governmental coercion.

Freedom is a sacred value—indeed, a necessity of human survival—which men have understandably fought and often died for over the millennia. Freedom means a man can choose his goals and work to gain them without coercive interference from either other private citizens or the state. It also means that he is responsible for his own life, for he who makes decisions must bear responsibility for them. The decision maker's thinking and action initiate the cause(s) that actuate all consequences. It is logical and just that when an individual makes the choices controlling his life, he reaps the rewards of positive choices and suffers the consequences of negative ones. All values worth having are gained by work and effort, and personally shouldering the responsibility of achieving them is in the nature of being free.

Freedom equals responsibility. Conversely, if someone else supports an individual, then to that extent he controls him. Parents provide for a child, and lay down rules of appropriate conduct in their home. Many teenagers, for example, have ruefully realized that their freedom to live as they would must wait until they decamp the nest and independently support themselves. Similarly, when the state provides for a man, it stipulates what is and is not permissible. It ensures that its money is spent in accord with its guidelines.

When the state provides medical care, for example, it, not the patient, selects the attending physician(s), the fee to be paid, and, in consequence of its policies, the date at which overloaded government doctors can finally take his case, if ever. Tragically, in practice, this means the state often decides who lives and who dies. A man dependent on the state is necessarily a ward of the state. His freedom is inevitably restricted to the extent the state supports and cares for him. In effect, he remains a child, with a nanny state now substituting for mother and father.

The solution is to recognize that an individual is morally responsible only for the choices he makes and not for any factor beyond his control. He is responsible for his own life, for his children, for any person he voluntarily chooses to support—and for no one else. Specifically regarding medical care, he is therefore responsible for paying the bills of himself, his children, anyone he voluntarily undertakes to care for—and nobody else.

Supporters of government medicine claim to feel compassion for human beings, but, by forcing some to provide for others, display a pitiless ruthlessness toward their coerced victims. Supporters of free market medicine, on the other hand, uphold not compassion but the principle of individual rights, thereby refusing to initiate force against the innocent. In respecting the rights of all men, they show far greater goodwill toward their fellow man, and are free to aid the needy via private, voluntary charity—which flourishes in America—including in the field of medicine.

In any field, a free market creates an abundance of low-priced, high-quality goods and services: this is true of food, shoes, cell phones, computers, automobiles, dish soap, pain relievers, hair stylists, plumbers, contractors, automotive repairmen, and a plethora of others. It is true of medical care, as well, as the history of American medicine prior to World War II demonstrates.

Conversely, government control of any field—from agriculture to steel making to education to health care—results in shoddy products and chronic shortages.

The rational conclusion must be: the more vital a good or service—the more human life requires it—the more urgent is the need of a free market to provide it. For medical care the level of urgency is high. Americans must identify this truth—and then make the right choice.

A free market of medicine respects the rights of all individuals, doctors as well as patients; consequently, it results in an abundance of affordable, high-quality medical care. Once again, on this issue as on so many others, the moral is seen to be the practical.

4

The Right to Abortion as an Application of Individual Rights

Notice that both sides in the abortion debate invoke the principle of "rights." Anti-abortionists claim to uphold a "right to life." Pro-choice advocates speak of a woman's "right to abortion." But neither side holds a rigorously defined theory of rights; in consequence, each side's arguments are woefully weak.

Most anti-abortionists are religious conservatives, whose view of human nature and rights is grounded in faith-based beliefs, bereft of rational arguments. Simultaneously, most pro-choice advocates are liberals who argue that a woman's "right" to choose is based in her subjective experience, in her feelings, not in an objective analysis of human nature and the nature of rights. Even the term liberals employ—pro-*choice*—shows support for a woman's "choice," regardless of whether a fetus has or has not objectively attained the status of human personhood.

Put simply: conservatives argue on the basis of faith; liberals from the standpoint of emotionalism. Both eschew reason—in general, and regarding this issue specifically.

But regarding any problem, and, above all, one so controversial, reason is the sole method by which to solve it.

In fact, a woman does have a right to choose between motherhood and abortion, although not for the irrational reasons advanced by liberals. The validation of a right to abortion requires a rational understanding of the concept "rights," a definition grounded in the facts of nature, neither in religious faith nor in subjective feeling.

As seen in Part One, "rights" are moral principles necessary to uphold and protect the life of a distinctively human being—i.e., an *individual of a rational nature.* These two factors form the logical foundation of the concept "rights": individuality—and a rational nature.

If the anti-abortion argument is critically examined, it becomes apparent that its supporters have no logical basis for the use of the phrase "right to life." In this, lies one of its fundamental errors. An analysis of the conservatives' errors can be employed to show that their appeal to the principle of a fetus' "rights" is logically groundless.

The conclusion of the anti-abortion argument is that abortion, at any point in the pregnancy, is murder; therefore, it must be outlawed. The fetus, they argue, is a human being from the moment of conception and therefore in possession of all moral and legal rights. The legal system, the anti-abortionists conclude, must protect the rights of the unborn.

The conventional argument against abortion is grounded in belief in the supernatural; in the history of the Platonic-Christian school of philosophy. Because the roots of the anti-abortion position lie in traditional Christianity, its continued appeal rests on this affinity to religion. The modern anti-abortionist view of human nature comes directly out of religious faith.

The philosophic father of this view was Plato. In his dialogue, "The Phaedo," Plato defined a human being as "a soul imprisoned within a body" and argued that "a true philosopher yearns for death." His theory emphasized a spiritual, supernatural component to human nature: a human being is essentially an immortal soul temporarily conjoined with the flesh, yearning for death as means to attain wisdom in a higher world. Saint Augustine, the first great philosopher of the Catholic Church, and philosophically a neo-Platonist, stressed this view when he defined man as "a soul using a body." In the religious tradition, a human being is a temporary mixture of body and immortal soul.

Given such a religious approach, a logical question is: When is the immortal soul combined with the flesh? The anti-abortionist's answer is: at the moment of conception. The religionist holds that God delivers the immortal soul into its tiny embryonic body at the instant that conception occurs. Therefore, since the fetus possesses the defining characteristic of human personhood from its first moment, it must be considered a human being throughout the pregnancy, and consequently in full possession of all legal rights. As a result, the deliberate termination of its life is murder and must be prohibited by the government of any civilized society. If human nature is defined in religious terms, then abortion at any moment of the pregnancy is murder.

Philosophically, the problems of this viewpoint are manifest. First, it is a purely subjective position, based in faith, without a shred of objective fact to substantiate it. There is no rational evidence for the existence of an immortal soul or a God, much less that God breathes such a soul into the fetus at conception. These are matters of blind acceptance. But on the basis of faith, one could accept anything: that burning bushes speak, men live inside whales, and virgins give birth—that the Pope is infallible—that God told Ayatollah Khomeini or Osama bin Laden to murder infidels—and that consuming meat on Friday or meat with dairy is sinful. Faith is a cognitive approach that lacks the ability to prove the truth of any of its claims.

But even aside from the arrant nonsense of such beliefs, there is a second, related point. This concerns the relationship of the legal system to cognition. The laws of a free society must be grounded in demonstrable fact. Where men are free to independently deploy their minds, the most rigorous thinkers will call for factual evidence and rational arguments grounded in it; the most logical arguments will win. This is the reason all dictators, religious or secular, always suppress freedom of intellectual expression—and incarcerate or execute independent thinkers; because they know that on a free market of ideas their arbitrary dictates will be found without logical basis.

The American Founders understood this point; children of the Enlightenment, such thinkers as Franklin, Jefferson, Paine et al., comprehended that man is a reasoning being holding an inalienable right to speak his mind, no matter the unpopularity of his sentiments. "I swear eternal hostility to all forms of tyranny over the mind of man," Jefferson stated, providing eloquent expression of the deep truth that rational beings must be free to speak and act in accordance with the judgment of their minds. If men are to be left free to think, then all arbitrary dogmas must be ruthlessly extirpated from the legal system.

But faith is a cognitive approach inimical to such freedom of thought; ultimately, if permitted into the legal system, it leads to authoritarianism, be it in medieval Europe, Calvin's Geneva, or the Ayatollah's Iran. This is because the purpose of religion is to subordinate men to God's law. If man's law—the law of the land—is to put into effect God's law, it must be directed by those most expert in interpreting God's will: the clergy and theologians. Religion is authoritarian in its essence: God stipulates and men obey. If such a method is allowed into a nation's legal system, its logical impetus toward theocracy constitutes an immense danger to liberty.

125

The unprovable in reason is and will always be the coercively commanded in politics. If you do not deal with men by reason, then you deal with them by force. There is no third alternative. This is the deepest reason the country was founded on a legal separation of state and church, and why this attempted separation must be upheld. A free society must not legislate the unprovable dogmas of faith.

In brief: the faith of the believer is irrelevant to the claim that an unformed chunk of tissue feeding off the life-support systems of a woman's body is a human being with all the rights thereof. In logic, the religious argument has no case: no evidence, no facts, no proof. Its premises are grounded in the arbitrary claims of faith, and, as such, are rationally untenable and to be dismissed. Above all, such beliefs must not serve as the basis of legislation by either federal or state authorities.

But in recent decades, anti-abortionists have presented a modern, scientific argument to supplement their traditional religious one. The evidence they point to consists of two biological facts: (1) The fetus is a living being; (2) The fetus has the genetic structure—the twenty-three pairs of chromosomes—characterizing human life. In short, biologically, a fetus is a living being that possesses the genetic makeup, not of a horse or a dog or a cat but of a human being.

John Noonan, an influential anti-abortion writer, makes the point this way in his widely reprinted essay, "An Almost Absolute Value in History": "The positive argument for conception as the decisive moment of humanization is that at conception the new being receives the genetic code. It is this genetic information which determines his characteristics, which is the biological carrier of the possibility of human wisdom, which makes him a self-evolving being. A being with a human genetic code is a man." Or as Noonan makes the point in simple eloquence elsewhere in his essay: "Anyone conceived by a man and a woman is human."

These claims about genetics are undeniable facts of science to which any rational person must accede. The question is not: Is the fetus alive? It is. Nor is the question: Does the fetus have the genetic code of a human being? It does. The question is: Are these qualities sufficient in themselves to certify the fetus as a human being? Granted that possession of such characteristics represents a necessary condition of being human, does it also represent a sufficient condition?

The answer, in logic, is an emphatic: No.

Early in the pregnancy—throughout the entire first trimester—the fetus is a tiny chunk of protoplasm, biologically unformed and dependent on the mother's life-support systems for the ongoing sustenance of its life. Early in the pregnancy, a fetus does not bear the remotest resemblance to the form of a human being; nor can it sustain its own biological functions: it is not the fetus' heart which pumps blood through its body—but the mother's; it is not the fetus' stomach which digests its food, but the mother's; it is not the fetus' brain which controls such life-support functions—but the mother's, etc.

In essence, a fetus in its early stages is not a biologically formed or individuated entity; it is a biological growth within the body of a host organism. It survives only as a biological dependency.

It is an undeniable truth that a fetus is a potential human being. But it is equally undeniable—rationally undeniable—that to be a human being requires an organically formed individuation. Part of a human being's fundamental nature is to be an individual; men are not biological dependencies feeding off the life-support systems of other living beings. Put simply, a human being is an entity, not a component. A state of full biological development is central to the attainment of individuation and to the achievement of human personhood.

This is an observational, not a theoretical point, that can be established ostensively, by pointing. There is an obvious, visually apparent difference between a fully formed, biologically developed individual—including an infant—and a tiny chunk of tissue living dependently within the body of another. One is recognizably human—and the other recognizably a mass of protoplasm. The obvious perceptual difference between these two life forms is one that even a child can see and understand. The anti-abortion thinker must come to grips with this argument. He must refute it if he is to make his case that human personhood begins at conception.

But the anti-abortion literature on this point is very weak. For instance, John Lippis, in his pamphlet, "The Challenge To Be Pro-Life," a piece of writing widely disseminated by the anti-abortion movement, counters it this way: "This decision [Roe vs. Wade] holds the child worthy of protection only if capable of existing by itself, ignoring the more fundamental need of this child—by the very nature of its youth—to be nurtured and cared for until he or she is *truly* viable. This independence, by any reasonable terms, does not come until late adolescence."

127

Noonan makes the exact argument: "The most important objection to this approach," he writes, "is that dependence is not ended by viability. The fetus is still absolutely dependent on someone's care in order to continue existence; indeed, a child of one or three or even five years of age is absolutely dependent on another's care for existence; uncared for the older fetus or the younger child will die as surely as the early fetus detached from the mother. The insubstantial lessening in dependence at viability does not seem to signify any special acquisition of humanity."

Both arguments rest on the logical fallacy of equivocation. Both cases rely upon a switch in meaning of the key terms "independent" and "dependent." The right-to-abortion side means by the term "independent"—to be *biologically* independent or self-sufficient, i.e., to be individuated, fully formed or developed, a single autonomous biological entity. But the anti-abortion side speaks of "independence" or "viability"—"true viability," as Lippis puts it—as full intellectual–emotional–financial independence, as being able to support and care for oneself as a mature, responsible adult. Based on this, the anti-abortionists conclude that "true viability" does not occur until late adolescence and therefore cannot serve as the criterion of human personhood.

But the truth is that to attain full intellectual–emotional–financial independence is irrelevant to the issue. Millions of human beings never achieve this. That is not the point. Independence in this context means one thing and only one: that human personhood requires a full organic development, to be a bodily individual, not a biological growth or dependency.

A human being is not an aspect of anything or anybody else; he is an individual.

This and nothing else is the issue, and the anti-abortion side needs to directly address it, not obscure it under piles of equivocations.

To emphasize: a biological growth living inside the body of another organism, whose life is biologically supported by that organism, is not yet a human being.

Some of the anti-abortion literature even identifies facts that emphasize exactly this point. For example, the pamphlet "A Christian Response to Abortion," circulated by the Catholic Archdiocese of New York, specifies that at eight weeks the fetus is merely three centimeters (one-and-one-eighth inches) long and weighs merely one gram (one-thirtieth of an ounce). To be blunt, no being weighing one-thirtieth of an ounce is yet a human being, regardless that under certain circumstances it will develop into one. One, though by no means the only, important error in the anti-abortion argument is this failure to distinguish between a potential human being and an actual one.

It is important in this context to bear in mind Aristotle's distinction between the potential and the actual. A thing is in a state of actuality when it has reached its full development; it is still in a state of potentiality when it has the capacity to reach that development but has not yet done so. So although an acorn can and will grow into an oak tree under the right circumstances, it is ludicrous to consider the acorn identical to the tree. A tree and an acorn differ in numerous respects that are observationally apparent. They differ in size, shape, weight, biological functioning, to name only a few. While it is accurate to describe the acorn as a potential oak, it is obviously mistaken to characterize it as an actual one.

The actuality of a living being requires, *as a minimal condition*, full possession of all of that organism's distinctive and developed characteristics, even if in a youthful state. So a sapling, a baby tree, may be considered an oak; just as an infant must be considered human; even though both exist in a youthful stage of development. But an unformed, nonindividuated fetus lacks even the minimal condition of an actualized human nature—a developed heart, lungs, brain, etc. It fails to possess *biological individuality*, a fundamental attribute of being human. Like an acorn, it lacks the remotest resemblance to a state of actuality.

Being potentially a thing does not make something actually that thing. If it did, we could live in a heap of bricks and cinder blocks, drive a pile of scrap iron and rubber, eat apple seeds or peach pits for a nutritious snack, and keep as a pet the clump of tissue living inside a female cat's womb. But we cannot. The growth inside a woman's body is no more a human being than that inside the feline's body is a cat. The fetus is certainly a potential human being, but, by that very fact, by existing merely in a state of potentiality, it is excluded from yet being an actual human being.

Given these facts, the deficiency of the genetic argument should be clear. It is true that the fetus has a human genetic code. But so does every cell in the body. When a person rubs his arm, he brushes off living cells that will then die. Does this make him a murderer? Are those cells human beings because they possess the human genetic code? Obviously, it is mistaken to think so.

129

Having a certain genetic code gives such cells the *potential* to be cloned into a human being. But the fetus, during the first trimester, is merely a clump of these cells, and ascription to it of human personhood is equally mistaken.

Ayn Rand pointed out: "If any among you are confused or taken in by the argument that the cells of an embryo are living human cells, remember that so are all the cells of your body, including the cells of your skin, your tonsils, or your ruptured appendix—and that cutting them is murder according to [this theory]...A proper definition of man would not permit anyone to ascribe the status of 'person' to a few human cells."

The rational conclusion is that human personhood requires individuation. Philosophers can argue regarding the exact moment human life begins. Is it during the last stages of pregnancy, when the fetus has achieved full biological development and has a capacity for individual life? Is it only at the moment of birth when the umbilical cord is snipped and the infant is actually individualized? This is a fascinating question—but is not relevant to the abortion question.

It is an egregious error in the abortion debate to switch the discussion away from the early stages of pregnancy and to its last moments. For, in fact, the third trimester is a nonissue. First, very few abortions are performed during this period. Second, for a woman suffering from health problems, it is as dangerous to abort at this stage as it is to give birth; so there are no medical reasons necessitating third-trimester abortions. Third, and central, a fetus does not achieve organic development until some time between the twenty-eighth and thirty-fourth weeks, *at the earliest*; so that even the minimal requirements of human personhood are absent through the first six months.

What is clear is that events of the third trimester—when the fetus' lungs reach full development, when the fetus gains weight, and increases in strength preparatory to birth—are irrelevant to the abortion issue. What is relevant, and essential, is the first trimester, a period during which it is unambiguously clear that the fetus is a biological dependency, and unquestionably not a human being.

Anti-abortionists raise a fascinating philosophic question regarding this point. They ask: how—by what process—does a fetus develop from merely "a clump of protoplasm" into a human being? How does such a momentous transformation occur? How can it? Observe the premise contained in the question. The belief is that unless a thing is X to begin with, it could not develop into X. The fetus must be human at the beginning, this argument goes, otherwise, it could not be human at the end. Human cannot come from nonhuman, a thing cannot derive from what it is not. Therefore, this argument concludes, it is at conception—at the beginning—when the fetus receives the genetic code, that it becomes human.

Notice that the argument denies the reality of change itself. Is it the case that a hodge-podge heap of steel and rubber is an automobile? That a bucket filled with carbon, oxygen, hydrogen, and other chemical elements is a living being? Clearly not. Yet the car is constructed out of steel and rubber. A living being is composed of carbon and other chemical constituents. In reality, in terms of material makeup, living comes from nonliving, car comes from noncar, and human from nonhuman. *Any* view of human gestation must recognize this fact, including the anti-abortionists'. For if the fetus becomes human only at conception, then sperm and egg cells, prior to conception, are not human—and the human embryo comes from what is nonhuman. Change is a real part of the world, and the change undergone by the fetus, from a tiny clump of cells to a human being, is undeniable.

Because of such considerations, it is impossible for a fetus to possess rights. It was shown above that both morally and legally the concept of "rights" applies only to human beings—to *individuals* of a rational nature; that such a being must be free to act on the judgment of his mind, his survival instrument; that in the absence of such freedom, he is left no means to survive; and that the moral principle of *individual* rights, legally upheld by a proper government, is the indispensable means of protecting such freedom.

The concept of "rights" arises from, and is rationally necessary, only in a social context where other human beings could conceivably interfere with an individual's freedom to act on his own grasp of reality. The concept could have no conceivable relevance to a man alone on a desert island. Rights are, as Ayn Rand defined them: "moral principles defining and sanctioning a man's freedom of action in a social context."

Observe that a right involves an individual's freedom to act in his own best interest, not a guarantee of support at someone else's expense; certainly not a clump of protoplasm's guaranteed access to someone else's bodily and life-support systems.

Morally, the concept of individual rights refers to the fact that an individual's survival is based on his freedom to act on his own thinking; politically and legally it empowers the government to act as the protector of that freedom.

Put bluntly, the concept of "rights"—of an individual's rights and of the "right to life"—is based on and applies solely to individual human beings in a social context. The concept is rationally inapplicable to plants, to animals, and to biological dependencies within a woman's body. The concept arises only from consideration of a rational individual's survival requirements and is therefore applicable only to such a being. Biological growths, even though potentially human, stand outside the rational meaning of the concept "rights."

In summary: an undeveloped fetus is a nonindividuated growth within a woman's body. It is not an individual human being, and, consequently, stands outside the facts which give rise and rational meaning to the concept of "rights."

A woman is an individualized human being with all the rights thereof; an unformed fetus is not. The facts here are perceptually self-evident. Further, the mother's fulfillment rests upon her freedom to act on her own thinking. If she judges that carrying the pregnancy to term is in her best interest, then so be it; if she judges that terminating the pregnancy is in her interest, then likewise. An individual's right to life, the freedom to guide one's actions by one's own mind, must be safeguarded within the legal system of a free society.

This is the philosophic basis of a woman's right to abortion.

This is why the anti-abortion side is not merely mistaken, but misnamed. Its proponents have no logical entitlement to the phrase "right to life"; this is the logical property of the right to abortion side. Many centuries ago, the Chinese philosopher, Confucius, uttered the trenchant statement: "See to it that things are called by their right names." This is of more than semantic significance. The logic of each side's stand must not be confused. The pro-abortion side protects a woman's right to her own body and her own life. The anti-abortion side forces her into involuntary servitude to the biological needs of a hunk of protoplasm. Which side defends the right to life of an individual human being?

A woman's right to abortion must be seen as one fundamental application of the broader principle of individual rights. A woman has a moral right to terminate an unwanted pregnancy only because all individuals, in general, have the right to pursue their own fulfillment and happiness, i.e., they have the right to live. Without the principle of individual rights consistently upheld, no rational case in support of abortion can be made.

This raises a deeper moral issue that must be understood in order to philosophically defend a woman's right to abortion. Does morality require that an individual sacrifice himself in order to serve the needs of others—or does he have the right to pursue his own personal goals in quest of his own happiness? Do others necessarily come before self—or can personal happiness come first before satisfying the needs of others? In terms of moral philosophy, the question is: must an individual live altruistically, sacrificing himself for other people—or has he the right to live egoistically, pursuing his own goals even in the teeth of opposition from significant others? The answer to this moral question holds profound consequences for the abortion issue.

If one holds that other persons come first, that it is an individual's duty to serve the needy, to sacrifice one's self to the weak and the helpless, then, based on such a premise, one will be led logically to the anti-abortion conclusion. Nothing on Earth is more weak or helpless than an unformed embryo; for it lacks not only a capacity to support itself financially, but, more fundamentally, it does not even possess an independent capacity to support itself biologically.

It is not an accident that most of those who oppose a woman's right to abortion in the United States are devout Christians who accept Jesus' teaching in the Sermon on the Mount that moral virtue is measured by the degree of one's willingness to serve the meek, the weak, the sick, and the helpless. The religionist's "family values" program, with its attendant anti-abortion component, is of one piece, flowing logically from the basic message of Jesus: a woman's role in life is to conceive, bear, give birth to, and nurture babies. It is her duty to serve the needs of these helpless little ones, even when—perhaps especially when—that little one is a biologically unformed embryo unable to survive without her body as its incubator. When sacrificial service to the needy is the criterion of moral value, then a fetus' claims are unbeatable. To its abundant and unending biological needs a woman's right to her own career, her own happiness, even her own body is to be sacrificed.

On the altruistic view, since the mother is formed, individuated, biologically independent—since she is healthy and strong—*because* of such virtues, not *despite* them—she incurs an unchosen and unending moral duty to the helpless growth in her uterus. No socialist variant of selfless toil "for the people" can ever be more consistently altruistic and self-sacrificial than this. This religious call to sacrifice a gender is the voice of the Dark Ages, with its contempt for science, its animus toward medicine, its abysmally low life expectancy, and, above all, its duty-bound, self-sacrificial ethics, re-born in twenty-first-century America.

If one is to uphold a woman's right to her own body, in principle, one must begin by upholding an individual's right to his/her own life. It is only the moral theory of egoism, proclaiming that an individual is not a sacrificial animal, that he has an "inalienable right" to seek his own happiness; that his moral purpose is to pursue his own fulfill-ment—not to serve the needs of the people, the race, the tribe, the state, or the biologically dependent; it is only this code of ethics that is capable of liberating a woman from the enforced shackles of family servitude and empower her to live her own life of achievement, success, and joy.

Observe how the exponents of sacrifice are united against the individual self: whether they uphold service to Society, which is held to be greater than the self; or to the fetus, which clearly is less; in either case, they subordinate man—an individual, personal, living man—to something else, making it impossible to live his own life. The religionists want to save the fetuses, the leftists want to save the polar bears and the "rain forests," but both agree: humans must sacrifice for the nonhuman, human beings must be compelled to live in servitude to lesser life forms.

It is only an ethics of egoism that liberates an individual from involuntary servitude and urges him to pursue his own self-actualization. Because of this, it is only the ethics of egoism that can provide the basis for a woman's right to her own life, her own happiness, and her own body—a right that includes the right to bear, nurture, and rear children if she so chooses.

Without an egoistic moral basis, it is impossible to defend the rights of an individual. Only when achievement, success, self-fulfillment, and personal happiness are held to be the proper ends of a man's life, and when duty, sacrifice, unchosen obligations, and servitude, are rejected, only then is it possible to uphold an individual's inalienable right to "life, liberty, and the pursuit of happiness."

The failure to understand and support the principle of individual rights, and the egoistic theory that serves as its underlying moral foundation, are the main causes of this country's gradually eroding political freedom. From both ends of the political spectrum, from conservatives and liberals alike, the rights of an individual are under persistent attack.

Typically, liberals, under the influence of Marxism, work to enslave men in the economic sphere, seeking massive regulation of business, imposition on working people of every imaginable social welfare scheme—and coercive re-distribution of income to finance such schemes. Typically, conservatives, under the influence of Christianity, work to enslave men in the sphere of personal morality, seeking to ban abortion, outlaw gay marriage, and enforce mandatory prayer.

Whatever noise conservatives make about upholding individual rights in the economic realm—however much they claim to support free markets and capitalism—their determination to enforce government control over a woman's body reveals their essence as anti-individualists and statists.

Is such criticism of religious conservatives mere exaggerated alarmism? In answer, examine the following example. It is an illustration of contemporary culture, drawn from a textbook popular in the field of nursing ethics in relatively recent years. As an example of a serious ethical problem, the authors present the following case: "Let us consider the question, 'Should a person with two healthy kidneys be forced to donate one of them to an otherwise healthy person who is in irreversible kidney failure?'...Any person seriously approaching the problem of whether a healthy person should be forced to donate a kidney will be puzzled. To save a life is a 'good' thing to do. To force surgery on an unwilling and healthy individual is a 'bad' thing to do. The person who is ill has a right to life. The person who is healthy has a right to bodily integrity." What is the morally proper course of action?

To any rational human being—and above all, to Americans who respect the principle of individual rights—the only "puzzling" issue is: how could such a question ever arise in a civilized society? Manifestly, it is a monstrous violation of individual rights to force a man into organ donation, regardless the innocence or worthiness of the intended recipient.

But observe the pronounced resemblance to the abortion issue. For if a woman does not possess the legally protected right to control the biological processes in her own uterus, then, in principle, what right has any man to his own bodily organs? If the state can prevent a pregnant woman from terminating an unwanted pregnancy, then what moral principle restrains it from turning any one into a coerced organ donor? Many males mistakenly think of abortion as "a woman's issue." Nothing could be further from the truth. The truth is that it is an issue for any one concerned with his own inalienable rights—and that it is the most fundamental issue of all—for if a woman does not have the right even to her own body, then, in principle, what rights do any Americans have?

In the absence of a right to his own body, can it plausibly be argued that a man has the right to his own mind? What if his mind tells him that the coerced "redistribution" of his kidney is hideously evil? He surely has no right to act on his thinking in the presence of the state's abominable violation of his body. And if he has no right to his own thinking, what happens to his freedom of speech? Or to freedom of religion? What of a right to his own business or savings or private property?

The right to property is the right to keep the product of one's own effort—the effort of one's mind and body. But if one has no right to one's own body, then nothing prevents the state from expropriating the product of its effort. And if one has no right to any of these things, what has then become of a human being's "right to life?"

Given a proper validation of a woman's right to abortion, the futility of the liberals' "pro-choice" view is apparent. No human being may be granted the right to choose murder. Only when the anti-abortionist's argument that a fetus is human from the moment of conception is refuted, does it become clear that a woman has the right to choose between abortion and motherhood. The logic of the case requires to first establish biological individuation as the criterion of personhood, then to ground a woman's right of choice in this foundation. To be pre-choice in the absence of such a base is to tear away the foundation of the right-to-abortion argument. To turn the anti-abortionist's point against them: the fundamental issue here is not the right to choose but the right to life. A woman has the right to life because she is an individual human being. An unformed fetus has no such right because it is not. A consistent application of the principle of individual rights entails a vigorous defense of the right to abortion.

5

The Superiority of Free Market Education to Government Schooling

American education is in shambles. One in three fourth-graders score below the "basic level"—the lowest-ranking deemed proficient—on the reading portion of the National Assessment of Education (NAEP) exams. Among low-income students, half score below that level. In some of America's larger cities, fewer than half the students earn a high-school diploma; in Detroit, only one quarter do. Roughly one million children drop out of school each year. Forty-five million Americans are marginally illiterate. Twenty-one million cannot read at all.

Such statistics indicate not merely the current state of American education, but a decades-long trend in educational deterioration. Since 1983, ten million Americans have reached twelfth grade without learning to read at a basic level. In 1986, the national test score average for eleventh graders taking the NAEP literature and history test was 54.5 percent correct on the history portion, and 51.8 percent correct on the literature portion. In 1995, a nationally administered history test found that only one student in ten was grade-level proficient in the subject; the majority failed to reach a basic level. In 1996, U.S. high-school seniors scored near the bottom on an internationally administered math exam. Andrew Coulson, in his 1999 book, *Market Education*, pointed out: "a recent nationwide assessment of math skills found that 'only 14 percent of eighth graders scored at the seventh-grade level or above'" and "fewer than half of twelfth graders can do seventh grade work in mathematics." In 2000, math students in America ranked below those in Malaysia, Bulgaria, and Latvia.

Why is education in America—the world's wealthiest, most advanced nation—so abysmally bad? A central reason is the existence of America's government-run schools.

The many problems with government schools include the way they are funded, their lack of competition and economic incentive, the fact that children are forced to attend them, the schools' unaccountability regardless of performance, and various other conflicts inherent in a school system based on force. Consider these in turn.

Local, state, and federal governments finance the government schools by seizing wealth from productive men, largely via property taxes, but also by means of sales and income taxes, both personal and corporate. Thus, the schools are funded not voluntarily, based on merit, but coercively, regardless of merit.

Indeed, on the premise that poor academic performance can be remediated primarily by increased spending, the schools receive progressively *more* money, not less, as they educationally regress. New York City in 2003, for example, in an attempt to improve the dismal academic performance of its government schools, increased spending by $7 billion, only to be dismayed by the results of the 2007 NAEP exams, showing meager improvement in some areas and deterioration in others.

The gradual worsening of the government schools imposes gradually heavier financial liabilities on the taxpayers who are forced to support them. The government says, in effect, "The schools are underperforming because we do not violate individual rights sufficiently; we must do so on an even wider scale."

For many families, the taxes they pay to support the government schools make it impossible for them to send their children to a private school, for they are financially unable to pay twice for education. Making matters worse, truancy laws mandate that children attend school until age sixteen. This combination of coercive policies means that many students are *forced* to attend government schools.

The current arrangement makes the government school system akin to a monopoly, in that it is impervious to competition.

By analogy, suppose the government established a state-run automobile company; legally required all adults to own a car, which they received "free" of charge; and, by means of property, sales, and income taxes, financed the government-car producer, thus making it monetarily impossible for millions of Americans to purchase a privately manufactured automobile. Such a "business" would gain its income and "customers" by means of a rights-violating system, and it would receive the same income and "customers" regardless whether its "customers" deemed its product satisfactory. The government-car producer would lack any and all economic incentive to excel; no matter how woeful its product, it would be kept in "business" by wealth taken coercively from taxpayers. This is what the government school system does in the realm of education.

Further, government schools create irresolvable conflicts regarding curricula, textbooks, and teacher training. In order for the government to ensure that its schools are providing government-quality education, the state must establish an agency—call it the Bureau of Education—to oversee the schools, curricula, textbooks, and teacher training. Who controls the Bureau? In a dictatorship, the government controls it and employs the state schools to ram propaganda down the throats of its subjects. In a mixed economy, such as America's, competing interest groups vie for control of the Bureau, seeking to impose their preferred educational standards on the nation's youth.

Consider just a few of the conflicts arising from the current American system. Some groups want schools to teach creationism; others want them to teach evolution. Some want schools to teach the "virtues" of socialism and the "crimes" of America; others want them to teach the virtues of freedom and the unprecedented accomplishments of America. Some want schools to teach that America is a Christian country; others want them to teach that America is a secular republic. Some want schools to teach the "look-say" or "whole-language" method of reading; others want schools to employ phonics.

Such conflicts follow logically from the coercive methods by which government schools are funded, populated, and operated.

By contrast, private schools entail none of these problems.

It is common knowledge that private schools are generally academically superior to government schools, and this superiority is borne out on various tests. For instance, in the area of reading, private-school fourth graders in 1994 scored nineteen points higher than their government school counterparts on the NAEP exam. Likewise, in the field of math, also during the 1990s, the disparity between private school and government school achievement, on average, over the course of high school, was equivalent to 3.2 years of learning. More recently, in 2008, educational researcher Andrew Coulson reported on a comprehensive study—analyzing twenty-five years of educational research from eighteen nations—that compared government schools to private schools. The analysis demonstrated not merely the academic superiority of private education, but, more revealingly, that "the private sector's margin of superiority is greatest when looking at the least regulated, most market-like private schools."

One school that demonstrated both the superiority of the private model and the problems posed for private schools by government schools was Westside Preparatory School in Chicago, founded in 1975 by Marva Collins. Collins was a schoolteacher in Chicago who, frustrated by the bureaucratic restrictions of the government schools, resigned and opened Westside Prep. She took in many low-income and minority children deemed incorrigibly uneducable by the same government schools she had fled and transformed them into consummate students.

She jettisoned the look-say and whole language methods of teaching reading used in the government schools, taught phonics instead, and made reading a vital part of every aspect of her curriculum, including mathematics. She did not organize classes based exclusively on age, but let students progress as rapidly as they were able, and used advanced students to assist in the teaching of novices. Both she and her school became justly famous for the academic excellence achieved by their students. Unfortunately, due to insufficient enrollment and funding, Westside Prep closed in 2008—while government schools in Chicago continued to receive both students and funding by means of coercion.

Countless comparisons of private schools to government schools reveal that the former generally outperform the latter. The question is: Why?

The main reason for private school superiority is that such schools are *immune* to the problems that inescapably plague government schools.

A private school cannot force customers to purchase its product, nor can it compel anyone to finance its existence, nor can it regulate or curtail the activities of its competitors. Because private schools are legally forbidden to use force, their existence and programs entail no violation of rights. Having to earn their customers and money, private schools possess strong economic incentive to provide excellent educational services. If they want to stay in business and flourish, they must make money by satisfying the educational requirements of students and their families; if they fail to do so, they face bankruptcy. (Even nonprofit private schools must compete for students and funding. If they fail to deliver a satisfactory educational product, families send their children to a competitor that does. And if they fail to succeed in their stated mission, their philanthropic financiers will find other venues for their magnanimity.)

Further, private schools pose no irresolvable problems of curriculum, textbooks, or teaching methods. The owners of private schools decide what subjects will be taught, the teaching methods to be employed, and the price at which their services will be offered. Parents voluntarily purchase the service for their children—or not—and continue to purchase only if satisfied with the educational result and its price.

If a private school chooses to teach the theory of evolution in its biology curriculum, it is free to do so, and potential customers are free to decide whether they want that for their children. If a different private school chooses to teach creationism, it is free to do so, and potential customers are free to choose *that* for their children. If a private school chooses to focus on the three Rs to the exclusion of painting, music, or drama, it is free to do so, and potential customers are free to patronize the school or not. If another private school chooses to focus on the arts—or trade skills—or to offer any variety of subjects—it is free to do so, and potential customers are at liberty to do business there or not.

The philosophy of education is a complex and controversial issue—and people's needs and values differ in countless ways. In a system of private schools, everyone is free to spend their money as they deem best—and to choose where he will educate his child; no one is compelled to finance schools he deems unworthy—or patronize ideas he deems false or pernicious.

In brief, private schools do not abrogate rights; consequently, are free of the myriad problems that inevitably accompany such violations.

Both morally and practically, private schools are superior to government schools.

History demonstrates this as fully as do current educational practices.

Prior to the mid-nineteenth century, government schools did not exist in America. All schools were private, and education was widespread and outstanding. For example, in the Middle Atlantic colonies during the pre-Revolutionary period, professional educators established numerous schools to satisfy the demand for education. Philadelphia, for example, boasted schools for every subject and interest. Between 1740 and 1776, 125 private schoolmasters advertised their

141

services in the city's newspapers—this in a town whose population was miniscule relative to today. Professional educators provided mentoring services in English, contemporary foreign languages, science, and a wide variety of other topics. Children who grew to be such brilliant scientists, writers, and statesmen as Benjamin Franklin, Thomas Jefferson, and George Washington received their education at home or in private schools.

(As to higher education, by the late-eighteenth century six private colleges operated in the colonies: Yale, the College of New Jersey [Princeton], the College of Philadelphia [Penn], Dartmouth, Queen's [Rutgers], and Rhode Island College [Brown].)

Predictably, the educational results of such a free educational market were superb. The literacy levels of Revolutionary America were remarkably high. For example, Thomas Paine's book, *Common Sense*, written in plain style but enunciating sophisticated political principles, sold 120,000 copies during the colonial period to a free population of 2.4 million (akin to selling 10 million copies today). The essays of *The Federalist*, written by Hamilton, Madison, and Jay in support of a Constitution for the nascent republic, were largely newspaper editorials written for and read by the common man.

Sales of American books and educational materials in the early-and-mid-nineteenth century likewise indicate a high national literacy rate. Between 1818 and 1823, while the U.S. population was under twenty million, Walter Scott's novels sold five million copies (the equivalent of selling sixty million copies today). Early in the nineteenth century, James Fenimore Cooper's *The Last of the Mohicans* likewise sold millions of copies. The *McGuffey's Readers*, first published in 1836, routinely used such terms as "heath" and "benighted" in third-grade texts. They asked such questions as "What is this species of composition called?" and gave such assignments as "Relate the facts of this dialogue." The fourth-grade reader included selections from Hawthorne, and the fifth-grade text, readings from Shakespeare. "These were not the textbooks of the elite but of the masses," explains Thomas Sowell. "[F]rom 1836 to 1920, *McGuffey's Readers* were so widely used that they sold more than 122 million copies."

Given the high quality of education in early America, it is no surprise that two renowned French visitors observed and reported on the phenomenon. In an 1800 book Vice-President Thomas Jefferson commissioned, titled *National Education in the United States of America*, Pierre Du Pont de Nemours reported that Americans received an education far superior to that of other peoples. "Most young Americans," he wrote, "can read, write, and cipher. Not more than four in a thousand are unable to write legibly." Several decades later, Alexis de Tocqueville wrote in *Democracy in America* that Americans were the most educated people of history.

Private schools in America have provided and continue to provide high-quality education.

Unfortunately, private schools today constitute less than 11 percent of America's educational system. According to the National Center for Educational Statistics, in school-year 2009–2010, nearly 49.8 million students attended government schools, while 5.8 million were enrolled in private schools. Because of the numerous coercive laws earlier discussed, almost 90 percent of American children are compelled to attend educationally crippling government schools. This is not merely a tragedy. It is a man-made tragedy; indeed, an atrocity.

What is the solution?

One key political solution to the abysmal state of education in America is to privatize the government schools. For an indication of what would happen to education in America if the government schools were privatized, consider the industries that are either fully or essentially private. Examine the quality, availability, and prices of automobiles, cell phones, CDs, MP3 players, jeans, breakfast cereals, and pain killers. Consider the quality, availability, and prices of services such as hair styling, car repair, plumbing, and dentistry. If focus is placed on any of these, it becomes apparent that the private ownership of the businesses involved is the factor driving quality up, prices down, and availability widespread.

For example, when was the last time anyone complained about a shortage of high-quality, low-priced cell phones? Observe that there are countless varieties of cell phones, optional features, and calling plans. Cellular service producers competing for business provide customers with sparkling new high-tech phones *free of charge* upon contracting to purchase their service. Just over a century ago, people had no telephone service. Now they receive a personal, portable phone—indeed, a technological marvel—for free. Why are cell phones and calling plans so inexpensive, technologically advanced, and abundant? The answer is that the industry is relatively free of government interference. Producers of goods and services in a free market know that if they provide quality products for reasonable prices, they will profit—and that if they do not, their businesses will founder.

143

The economic bottom line is that if a producible good or service is in demand in a free market, profit-seeking businessmen will endeavor to supply it at affordable prices. Education is no exception.

In a fully privatized, free market of education, profit-seeking businessmen would provide quality educational services at prices affordable to millions. And because they would have to meet consumer demand in order to thrive, businessmen would provide a sweeping diversity of services matching actual student needs. For example, observing that many people value the full academic curriculum and want their children to learn the classic three Rs of reading, writing, and arithmetic, entrepreneurial educators would provide such a service effectively and affordably. Likewise, observing that many of these same people want their children to advance to science, mathematics, literature, and history, educators would provide these services, as well, because they could make money doing so.

The same is true of vocational training. Some families demand only the basics of academics, and then want their children to branch out into one of many vocational fields—whether business, farming, baking, construction work, or countless other productive fields. In a free market, profit-seeking educators would provide such services as efficiently and inexpensively as possible—lest competitors provide a better value and put them out of business.

This truth applies also to the field of special education. Some individuals require specialized instruction. For example, some are gifted in specific ways—intellectually, musically, athletically—and require highly focused, advanced training. Others suffer from debilitating psychological or physiological ailments. Some are sadly afflicted with varying degrees of mental retardation. In a free market, where there is a demand for various forms of special education, profit-seeking businessmen will compete to supply them.

All the data culled from the current state of education, from history, and from the logic of economics points without exception to a single conclusion: private schools competing for profits in free (or freer) markets produce quality, affordable educational services to satisfy customer demand.

Politically speaking, the practical solution to America's educational problems is to privatize the government school system—to convert the government schools into private schools. The reason this is the practical solution is because it is the moral solution. A fully private school system would recognize and respect the rights of everyone involved. It would leave educators and customers fully free to produce and purchase educational services in accordance with their own needs and preferences.

There are several objections to privatization that must be answered.

One objection is that there are some parents who do not sufficiently value their children's education to pay for it. To the extent that there are such parents, this is hardly a reason to violate the rights of all Americans and destroy the possibility of a good education for millions of other children. People who have children and do not care enough to educate them should be socially ostracized and, when appropriate, prosecuted for parental neglect. But they should not be held up as a reason to violate the rights of millions of Americans and to keep U.S. education in the sewer.

The fact is that the overwhelming preponderance of parents value their children's education enormously, and, when left free to spend their money as they deem best, would procure that value for their children, just as they do food, clothing, shelter, and medical care. Observe in this regard, the current trend toward homeschooling in America. An increasing number of parents, now more than a million, value their children's education so much and are so dissatisfied with government schools that they have chosen to home school their children—despite the fact that they are still forced to finance the government schools they do not use. (Not surprisingly, the educational results achieved by homeschoolers are generally outstanding. For example, by eighth grade most home-schooled children test four grade levels above the national average.)

If parents choose not to provide their children with a proper education, that is their right—and the children will, for a time, suffer the consequences of their parents' irrationality. But children are not mindless replicates of their parents; as they grow into adulthood, they can and often do make fundamentally different choices. For example, the children of religious parents sometimes choose secularism; the offspring of bigoted parents often choose individualism; and the children of alcoholic or drug-addicted parents often choose clean living. Human beings possess free will, and, as numerous parents ruefully learn, their children frequently do not passively accept their families' values.

Even in today's government-thwarted education market, many centers of adult education prosper. A fully free market in education would enable educational entrepreneurs to expand this market immensely. Competition among private schools and tutors providing both academic and vocational training for the adult market would increase; prices would drop; options would abound. In such a marketplace, the few children whose backward parents had neglected to educate them could seek education on their own in their early years of adulthood, then move on and live lives of greater wisdom and increased career opportunities.

Finally, it is important to emphasize that there is no right to an education—just as there is no right to food, shelter, or medical care. A right involves the freedom to act on one's best judgment and to pursue the values of one's choice. It does not involve access to a good or service at someone else's expense. If a person (or a citizenry) is forced to provide others with education (or anything else), then his rights are violated and he becomes, to that extent, a slave of those he involuntarily serves. A free market in education would both obviate such manifest immorality and provide immensely better options in all educational fields.

Another objection to a fully privatized educational system is that if taxpayers were not coerced to finance government schools, some families would be unable to afford quality education. The first response to this objection is that the coercively funded and operated government schools are precisely what makes it impossible for customers to receive quality education. Another important point is that with the government monolith slain, the property, income, and sales taxes that had been levied to sustain it could and should be repealed. With their tax burden substantially diminished, families would retain more of their income and be fully free to spend it on their children's education. Further, in a full private market for education, competition among private schools, teachers, and tutors would increase dramatically. This would inevitably drive prices down, making education increasingly affordable.

For those families who, even in a free market, could not afford to pay for education, bear in mind that even today many private schools offer scholarships to worthy students who cannot meet the tuition. In a fully free market for education, such scholarships would increase and abound. Private schools are highly competitive with one another; they seek to showcase the value and superiority of their product. As a result, it is in their rational self-interest to attract students who will make them shine. Scholarships are an important means of doing so.

It is worth noting that voluntary charity flourishes in America despite the obscenely high tax rates of the current day. According to Giving USA Foundation's annual report on philanthropy, "Charitable giving in the USA exceeded $300 billion for the second year in a row in 2008,"—and "Education organizations received an estimated $40.94 billion, or 13 percent of the total." So long as the government does not prohibit educational charities, Americans will contribute to such a worthy cause.

In short, in a fully private market for education, the few families unable to afford quality education would find no shortage of scholarships and/or charities available to assist them. There exist no valid objections to privatizing the government schools.

(A question that might be raised is: why are government schools in other countries often superior to government schools in America? Although this is a fascinating question to research and answer, it avoids the fundamental issue. Since, for the reasons provided, a free market of education is substantially superior to government schooling, the most important question is: how much better would the educational systems be in these other countries were they to institute a free educational market?)

By what method could the government schools be privatized?

There are several viable means by which this could be done—but the simplest, most straightforward way is to auction off schools and their properties to the highest bidders. Sold schools would either continue under private ownership, or the properties would be used for noneducational purposes. If such properties became private schools, competition in a free market would ensure a drive toward improved education and decreased prices. If some of the properties were deployed for noneducational purposes, the resultant increased demand for education in that area would motivate profit-seeking educational entrepreneurs to meet the demand at other venues. Either way, the market would soon teem with private schools, teachers, and tutors competing to supply the educational service demanded by millions of families whose only earlier alternative was the abysmally bad government school system.

Such a major transition would necessarily take time: the government would have to provide fair notice and an appropriate grace period to enable government-dependent families to adjust to a free market. For example, the government could enact a law declaring that, effective immediately, the state would begin auctioning off school properties, with transference of ownership to occur at the end of a five-year grace period. This would enable all teachers, tutors, and educational entrepreneurs to ramp up their businesses; additionally, it would give all parents substantial time to assume full responsibility for the education of their children.

The enactment of such a policy would be followed by an explosion of private schools and tutoring services, many small-scale, some large; many in private homes—as Marva Collins began—some in multistory buildings; some religious, some secular; some profit-driven, others not. The teeming diversity of schools and the high level of educational results would soon rival those of America in the centuries before the imposition of government schooling.

Those who recognize the vital nature of education to the lives of individuals and the health of a society must demand the privatization of government-run schools and work toward the establishment of a fully free market in education. The time to advocate such change is now.

6

Individual Rights Applied to Representative Issues

Although the issues examined above are the nation's most urgent, there are other lesser but still significant problems to be resolved. The ones briefly analyzed in this chapter are: the right to bear arms, the war on drugs, immigration, and gay marriage. All four involve the principle of individual rights under persistent attack from various statist factions, whether conservative or liberal.

The Right to Bear Arms

Every honest man and woman should own a gun, know how to use it, and be prepared to use it in defense of their own lives, and that of their loved ones or families.

Honest persons will then be safer, and the crime rate will drop significantly. Logical reasoning and the empirical data combine to make an overwhelming case in support of this conclusion.

The moral argument is manifest. An honest man, committing no initiation of force or fraud against others, has the right to own a gun for any reason he chooses: whether for home protection, or hunting, or collecting, or any other. The government must be granted no jurisdiction to dictate to honest, consenting adults what they may be permitted to do regarding any issue, gun ownership or any other. No innocent individuals are threatened by guns in the hands of honest men; indeed, in cases of criminal assault, they are safer, for such ownership increases the likelihood of armed good Samaritans coming effectively to their aid.

Related: any honest person possesses a moral right to self-defense. If an individual possesses an inalienable right to his own life—as he does—then he necessarily possesses a right to defend his life against those brutes who would initiate force against him. Further, since his life and the means to defend it are his, he has the moral right to delegate to another honest man the responsibility of defending him from criminal assault. Therefore, when an innocent victim cries for help, or even when he struggles silently, every good Samaritan has the moral right to defend him. The victim's right to live free of violent onslaught, not the specific edicts of the legal system, constitute the moral basis of private aid to those suffering aggressive assault. The most effective current technology to facilitate self-defense against violent assailants—especially against those bigger, stronger, and/or armed with a dangerous weapon—is a gun.

The practical point should be obvious with just a few minutes of careful thought. Economist John Lott's book, *More Guns, Less Crime*, is the most carefully researched, definitive work on the practical effects of gun control. One point he makes, perhaps surprising to some, is that an overwhelming preponderance of sheriffs and police chiefs favor possession of guns by trained, qualified, honest men and women. For example, in a 1996 poll conducted by the National Association of Chiefs of Police, 93% of responding members said they favored guns in the hands of honest men for purposes of self-defense.

The reason is that honest cops know that too often they cannot prevent violent crime; in many cases, the best they can do is investigate one after its perpetration. Richard Stevens' chilling book, *Dial 911 and Die*, documents this heartbreaking truth. No matter how conscientious and determined, *the police cannot be everywhere.* It may take them mere minutes to respond to a 911 emergency call—*but a violent crime may be committed in mere seconds.*

Richard Mack, former sheriff of Graham County, Arizona, stated regarding Stevens' book: "How I wish that the information in this book were not true...Nevertheless, this book speaks to the irrefutable truth: *police do very little to prevent violent crime.* We investigate crime after the fact."

Gun control laws may well keep guns out of the hands of honest men—for they do not wish to break the law. But it is impossible—literally not possible—to keep guns out of the hands of criminals. For example, areas with extremely stringent gun control laws—New York City, Chicago, Washington, D.C., Detroit—have extremely high rates of crime, including gun crimes. The reason that anti-gun laws do not prevent criminals from procuring guns is complex, but may be stated simply: economically, when there exists demand for a product—desire backed by purchasing power—money can be made by supplying it. There will then be—have been, continue to be, will eternally be—many outlaws seeking to gain wealth by supplying the banned product.

Guns will remain—have remained, continue to remain, will always remain—plentiful.

For example, how many gun laws will it take to prevent criminals in New York, Detroit, Washington, D.C., or anywhere from purchasing so-called "Saturday night specials," i.e., small inexpensive handguns? The answer is: no amount of gun laws will achieve this purpose.

Did Prohibition prevent Americans from purchasing alcohol? Does the current War on Drugs prevent them from procuring illicit substances? No, such draconian laws did not, do not, and cannot. What such legislation "accomplishes" is to remove alcohol, drug, and/or gun trafficking from legitimate businessmen and place it in the hands of criminals. A rising murder rate is inevitable as rival violent gangs vie for control of territories that assure profitable sales.

Morally, the point is a question of values. Criminals, by definition, are those willing to break the law. Some are willing to perpetrate assault, rape, and murder. If they are willing to commit such heinous crimes, will they be deterred by criminalizing the purchase of guns?

It is impossible to prevent procurement of X by criminalizing the purchase or ownership of X. Prohibition, the War on Drugs, and the strict gun laws in high-crime areas are tragic illustrations of this principle. Regarding guns, the tragedy is at its worst.

Gun control laws disarm honest men, making them vastly more vulnerable to assault by violent criminals. They diminish enormously the risk of perpetrating crime. Criminals are often cowards and bullies who seek the weakest prey possible, e.g., women and the elderly. When honest men and women have the right to own guns, the risk that a potential victim might effectively defend himself rises dramatically, making criminals significantly warier to strike. A good deal of empirical evidence exists to validate this claim.

For example, take the problem of so-called "hot" burglaries—in which the perpetrator breaks in while people are at home. Richard Poe points out in his book, *The Seven Myths of Gun Control*, that in America, where gun control laws are relatively lax, hot burglaries " account for only 13 percent of all U.S. burglaries." John Lott explains that an overwhelming preponderance of American burglars are careful to pick empty homes to rob. They sedulously avoid late-night burglaries, because as many convicted felons have stated to researchers: "that's the way to get shot."

But in such countries as Canada and England, with much stricter gun control laws, the rate of hot burglaries approaches 50 percent.

151

The obvious reason is that burglars know homeowners are legally disarmed; armed perpetrators can break in with impunity, putting at risk homeowners and their families.

Another point is the reduction in violent crime achieved in states permitting honest citizens to carry concealed hand guns. In reporting results of his comprehensive study, Lott states: "National crime rates have been falling at the same time as gun ownership has been rising. Likewise states experiencing the greatest reduction in crime are also the ones with the fastest growing percentage of gun ownership." Further: "the largest drops in violent crime from legalized concealed handguns occurred in the most urban counties with the greatest populations and the highest crime rates."

Richard Poe's report of Lott's findings is worth quoting at length: "...the violent crime rate dropped by 4 percent for each 1 percent increase in gun ownership. The most dramatic improvements came in states that allowed citizens to carry concealed handguns. States enacting such laws between 1977 and 1994 experienced an average 10 percent reduction in murders and a 4.4 percent drop in overall violent crimes during that period."

Lott, an economist, concludes: "...criminals as a group tend to behave rationally—when crime becomes more difficult, less crime is committed." This point must be amended, considering the arrant irrationality of criminal behavior. The conclusion stated more accurately is: criminals, as a group, tend to be *cowardly*—when crime becomes more dangerous, less crime is committed. Revealing is the statistic that in 98 percent of reported cases the perpetrator flees when he sees that his intended victim is armed—*and that no shots are fired.*

A related point involves the higher survival rate of individuals actively resisting criminal assault with a gun. The anti-gun crowd claims that the best way to survive criminal attack is by means of "active compliance"—to do exactly as the criminal says, as quickly as possible. This is false. The statistics (and a modicum of reasoning) show that the best way to survive criminal assault is by active resistance with a gun. This is especially true for women.

Gary Kleck examined data from the Department of Justice National Crime Victimization Survey from 1979 to 1987. Richard Poe succinctly reports his findings: "Women were 2.5 times as likely to suffer serious injury if they offered no resistance than if they resisted with a gun." The findings regarding men were less dramatic, but supported the same conclusion. "Men who offered no resistance were 1.4

times more likely to be seriously hurt than those who resisted with a gun."

The modicum of reasoning involved is that persons who own and know how to use a gun are immensely more equipped to defend themselves than a person unarmed. Effective self-defense offers the victim a significantly greater chance of safety than placing himself helplessly at the mercy of a violent thug.

A further point is the case of the Swiss. Perhaps no citizenry in the world is as heavily armed as are they. The country requires that every able-bodied man between ages twenty and forty-two serve in its militia. Richard Poe wrote: "Swiss law requires its citizen soldiers to store their gear at home, ready for action. Every man keeps a Sturmgewehr 90 assault rifle with ammunition in his closet." Additionally, militiamen are permitted to retain their rifles when retired from active service. When the Swiss Government updated its military rifles, it sold off the older ones to private citizens. Ammunition is sold by the government to private individuals at cost, to encourage target practice. Unbelievably to Americans, David Kopel, in his book, *The Samurai, the Mountie, and the Cowboy*, reported that the Swiss Government auctioned off to the public machine guns, howitzers, anti-tank weapons, cannons, and anti-aircraft guns. Richard Poe stated flatly: "...Switzerland remains the most heavily armed nation on earth, per capita..."

It is also one of the most peaceful nations on earth. In 1997, its murder rate was 1.2 homicides per 100,000 people, significantly lower than that in England, Canada, Australia, and New Zealand.

The anti-gun lobby will point out that Swiss culture stresses nonviolence, that even possession of machine guns, bazookas, and howitzers will not turn the Swiss into criminally aggressive thugs, and that the nation's policy of massive gun ownership will not work in countries whose cultures do not similarly emphasize the moral virtue of pacific nonaggressiveness. This, however, is precisely the point:

> Possession of deranged values, not possession of guns, is the cause of violent crime.

Imagine a country with a citizenry vastly more aggressive than Switzerland's, where, by divine intervention (which is what it would take) the government succeeded in keeping guns out of criminal hands. Would there be reduced violent crime? There would certainly be fewer gun crimes. But criminals, knowing that their victims possessed no guns, would then commit violent crimes using knives, blackjacks, clubs, garrotes, fists, poison, and even automobiles; this is especially true against the favorite targets of criminals: women and the elderly.

As a practical point: will violent criminals long survive in a country where virtually every honest man owns, is trained to use, and keeps in his home a military assault rifle?

Ownership of guns by honest men reduces violent crime; and, a related virtue: makes it far more likely that, in the event of confrontation, it is the perpetrator, not his intended victim that suffers bodily harm or death.

The converse point is also true: the more stringently gun control laws are imposed and enforced, the less likely it is that honest men will possess firearms with which to defend themselves. The rate of violent crimes, including gun crimes will then increase, as armed thugs know that they can assault their victims with virtual impunity. This point is demonstrated not merely by the high crime rates in U.S. cities with the most draconian gun laws, but by relatively recent events in both Britain and Australia.

In Britain, the Firearms Act of 1997 wrought the ban and confiscation of all handguns and most rifles. Predictably, a terrifying crime wave swept the country. Richard Poe provides the grim details: "Between April and September 2000, street crime in London rose 32 percent over the same period in 1999." In January of 2000, a *Sunday Times* of London article "reported an epidemic of gun crimes in London, Birmingham, and Manchester, fueled by a 'steady flow of smuggled guns from eastern Europe.'" Again from Poe: "The Home Office reported a 10 percent rise in gun crime in 1998. And in 1999-2000, crimes using handguns hit a seven-year high in Britain."

The same problem resulted in Australia. After a 1996 atrocity resulted in the murder of thirty-five innocent persons, the Australian Government banned most guns. More than 640,000 firearms were confiscated from honest men and women. Violent crime again rose dramatically.

Again from Richard Poe: "In the two years following the gun ban, armed robberies rose by 73 percent, unarmed robberies by 28 percent, kidnappings by 38 percent, assaults by 17 percent, and manslaughter by 29 percent."

No doubt startling to anti-gun activists, according to figures released in 2001 by the International Crime Victims Survey of Leiden

University, among industrialized nations Australia ranked number one in violent crime and Britain a close second. Fully 30 percent of Australian citizens had been victimized by violent crime; in Britain, the number was 26 percent, more than a quarter of its total population. Not surprisingly, the United States did not rank in the top ten of this shameful list.

Anti-gun adherents respond by demanding a worldwide ban on guns, thereby obviating the problem of gun smuggling from one nation to another. Such a policy, they believe, will keep guns out of criminal hands.

In reality, however, such a series of laws will work as effectively as a worldwide ban on alcohol, drugs, tobacco, or any other product. Again, the demand for guns means that great sums of money can be gained by supplying them. A vast black market will then spring up for stolen and smuggled military weapons from armed forces across the world. Further, the product of illicit gunsmiths in every nation will yield them great profits; and when one is apprehended and jailed, more will spring up to take his place; just as incarceration of one drug ring leads inevitably to the rise of another. There will occur the same hideous violence between rival gun smuggling rings as there exists currently between drug runners, and, in the past, between alcohol bootleggers.

The problem of crime is a problem of moral values, not one of gun ownership. Of absolute necessity is that moralists, politicians, parents, teachers, and the general populace come to realize Ayn Rand's principle that the initiation of force, in any form, is evil. This moral absolute, validated in the earlier philosophy section, must be restated here. The initiation of force, in any of its hideous iterations, not gun ownership, is what must be universally banned. The solution is to educate people to a rational philosophy—not to violate the inalienable rights of honest men.

A final point is that the right to self-defense includes that against dictatorial governments, not merely private criminals. Every tyrant seeks to disarm his subjects, leaving them physically defenseless against the assassins composing his secret police. For example, Richard Poe reminded us that in the Jim Crow south, Ku Klux Klan thugs and state militiamen "systematically ransacked the homes of black people, confiscating their weapons," leaving them helpless against the murderous depredations of racist brutes.

Further, one of the many horrible atrocities committed during World War II, was the mass murder of 34,000 Jews by Nazi troops at Babi Yar, Ukraine, in September 1941. As citizens of the Soviet Union, by Stalins' decree, and then by Hitler's conquering army, the Jews were legally prohibited from owning weapons. Did the strict legal ban on gun ownership imposed by the two dictators aid the Jews' attempt to survive—or make it impossible?

By contrast, the 1990s book and subsequent film, *Defiance*, told the true story of the Bielski brothers, armed Polish Jews who formed a band of freedom fighters, took refuge in heavy forest lands, rescued Jews of all ages, and remorselessly fought the Nazis. By war's end they were credited with saving the lives of more than 1,200 innocent persons, and killing hundreds of German troops in the struggle. Did possession of firearms by the Bielski brothers and their supporters hinder their attempt to survive Nazi aggression—or make it possible?

Stated Hitler in 1942: "History teaches that all conquerors who have allowed their subject races to carry arms have prepared their own downfall by doing so." Even Hitler might say something that is true. If oppressed peoples have weapons, they might conceivably rise up against a murderous tyrant; in the absence of such, they are helplessly doomed.

Rudolph Rummel, in his chilling 1994 book, *Death by Government*, coined the term "democide," meaning "murder of the people." His research involved solely the slaughter of unarmed civilians by dictators worldwide. He wrote: "In total, during the first eighty-eight years of [the 20th] century, almost 170,000,000[!] men, women, and children [have been murdered] in...the myriad ways governments have inflicted death on unarmed, helpless citizens or foreigners."

David Kopel made the excellent point that, "If only the government has guns, only the people the government cares to protect are safe." If the government does not care to protect blacks or Jews or dissidents or any other individual or group, then they are placed irrevocably in harm's way.

Such examples, and many similar ones, may be thought of as "death by gun control."

By contrast, the ragtag eighteenth-century American Minutemen, owning and proficient in the use of muskets, fought to a standstill the mighty British army. Similarly, many black American southerners were able to effectively defend themselves against murderous racists—including, at times, officials of the local governments—by their possession of, and expertise with firearms.

Richard Poe reminded us that in the Jim Crow south of the 1960s: "Civil rights workers...were often protected by armed patrols of the Deacons for Defense and Justice—a private black militia based in churches, with chapters in more than 60 southern cities." Benjamin Salter, a professor and NAACP organizer, wrote: "No one knows what kind of massive racist retaliation would have been directed against grassroots black people had the black community not had a healthy measure of firearms within it." Former Secretary of State, Condoleezza Rice, said her father, a minister, and his friends, armed themselves to effectively defend the black community against the violently racist White Knight Riders in Birmingham, Alabama, in 1962 and 1963.

Such examples, and many similar ones, may be thought of as "life by the right to bear arms."

As explained in the prior section on Ayn Rand's philosophy, *the moral is the practical.* When the inalienable moral right of an honest man to own and defend his life with guns is protected, the incontrovertible practical result is that many more innocent men will live longer, healthier lives.

(As the author writes this in January 2011, the murderous shooting spree of Jared Lee Loughner that killed six innocent victims and wounded many more, including Congresswoman Gabriele Giffords, incites the inevitable call for stricter gun laws. But this atrocity does not alter the moral and economic principles already discussed in this book. Guns will always be readily available to vicious murderers like Loughner; and strict gun bans will always lead to more violent crime against legally disarmed honest citizens. Several facts should be borne in mind in this context: (1) Arizona, where handguns are freely bought at gun stores and popular gun shows—and where ammunition is openly sold and bought at Wal-Mart—has a rate of violent crime *slightly lower* than the national average. (2) This lower rate of violent crime is achieved despite the hideous violence of the illegal drug trafficking that occurs along its border—murders that are a direct result of the misguided U.S. War on Drugs, described immediately following. What would greatly lower Arizona's rate of violent crime? Continue to staunchly protect the right of honest individuals to own guns—and legalize drugs, thereby removing drug trafficking from the hands of rival gangs of violent thugs and placing it under the control of honest businessmen, as with the end of alcohol Prohibition in 1933.)

It may be currently hopeless to convince many moralists and politicians of the manifest virtues of widespread gun ownership. But most honest men and women in the United States—and certainly in Switzerland—realize two vital truths: (1) It is the moral right of every upright person to own any gun he chooses—and to use it in defense of his own life or any other innocent person against violent assault. (2) Gun ownership by honest persons both reduces violent crime—and, in the event of such crime, makes it less likely that the victim suffers any harm. Such a realization, at least, provides a foundation upon which to build in the struggle to protect the right to bear arms and to defeat any and all attempts at legalized gun control.

The War on Drugs

The war on drugs must forcefully continue.

Drugs kill people—of that there may be no doubt. Cocaine in any form, heroin, ecstasy, LSD, and a host of other drugs are deeply toxic and extremely hazardous to health and life itself. Other drugs, less toxic—alcohol, marijuana, tobacco—may be used in moderation without serious harm; but, if abused, will engender physical and/or psychological dependency, and in time, premature death.

No rational human being wants to kill himself on toxic drugs, and no human being of even a modicum of good will desires to witness his otherwise innocent brothers and sisters kill themselves on such substances.

This is the reason a war on drugs must continue full throttle, indeed, be immensely accelerated.

The first step of a proper, rational, effective war on drugs is to fully legalize all drugs, including the most toxic, for the use of consenting adults. Full legalization is a necessary preliminary step in an intensified and ultimately victorious war on drugs.

It should now be apparent to all rational men that the government's War on Drugs is a colossal failure.

Here are the reasons supporting this conclusion.

Point one: It is horrifically immoral to coercively prevent adults from indulging their drug(s) of choice. Such a policy is a manifest violation of an individual's right to his own life, his own body, his own mind, and his own choice of which substance(s) to ingest into his body.

In a free country, based on a principle of inalienable individual rights, it is morally obscene for the criminal justice system to harass, arrest, and/or incarcerate an individual for mere possession, sale, or personal use of drugs. Objectively, where is the crime in such activities? None of these involve the initiation of force or fraud against another man. In no case of such victimless activities does an innocent individual require protection from criminal assault.

Morally, it is not the prerogative of the government to inquire into the substances consumed by consenting adults. The use of toxic drugs is indubitably self-destructive, and, as such, a serious vice—but vices are not identical to crimes. A crime always involves the initiation of force or fraud against another man; many vices do not. If the government equates vice with crime, then it can imprison adults for the mere use of alcohol, marijuana, and/or other drugs—and it has and does. Consequently, what moral principle then constrains the state from similarly incarcerating persons for consumption of tobacco, trans-fats, deep-fried foods—or anything else that will demonstrably endanger their lives? A fat-laden diet combined with a lack of exercise undoubtedly kills many more individuals than moderate use of beer, wine, or marijuana. If a government criminalizes vices, what moral principle restrains it from incarcerating obese, indolent sloths?

One is tempted to (futilely) cry out at the nanny state: "Laissez-faire! Leave it be!" These are matters that—among consenting adults—must be left to personal discretion. Thousands of U.S. citizens are currently in prison for the mere possession, sale, or personal use of banned drugs—and *the sole crime involved is the government's initiation of force against innocent individuals.*

Point two: the necessary consequence of flagrant immorality is flagrant impracticality. For example, to finance three decades of a massive War on Drugs, the government has spent an immense fortune. Economist, Jeffrey Miron, wrote in his 2004 book, *Drug War Crimes*, "In recent years government expenditure for prohibition enforcement has exceeded $33 billion annually..." Miron estimated that $7.7 billion is yearly spent enforcing prohibition of marijuana alone. Arnold Trebach, in his 2006 book, *Fatal Distraction*, cited official figures showing that between early 1993 and the end of 2003, the government spent in excess of $179 billion in its attempt to enforce drug prohibition laws. According to the Office of National Drug Control Policy (ONDCP), the total spent by federal and state authorities in their continuing anti-drug crusade exceeded $48 billion in 2010.

What has government accomplished by means of this expenditure of hundreds of billions of tax-extorted dollars? Has the War on Drugs effectively diminished the supply of toxic drugs to American users?

It has not. After this colossal expenditure, and after incarceration of countless individuals for the victimless "crime" of drug possession or use, *the availability and consumption of prohibited drugs in the United States is, to put it mildly, widespread—and is not declining.*

Trebach employed the government's own official figures to support this point. For example, in 2000, the ONDCP estimated that between 1989 and 1998, American drug users spent roughly $39 to $77 billion annually on cocaine, and $10 to $22 billion yearly on heroin. In 1998, Americans spent an estimated $11 billion on marijuana. In 2004, roughly two hundred metric tons of cocaine entered the United States. In 2010, ONDCP celebrated a 2009 decline in U.S. cocaine users—*to 1.6 million*—while downplaying its own admission of "overall increases in the use of other drugs."

Several years ago, the U.S. Office of Management and Budget concluded in calm understatement: "DEA [Drug Enforcement Administration] is unable to demonstrate its progress in reducing the availability of illegal drugs in the U.S."

There are both economic and moral reasons for such abysmal failure; indeed, *reasons that necessitate such failure.*

The same economic principles that apply to guns apply to drugs too. If substance X is in demand, i.e., is desired by many who can afford to purchase it, then money can be made by supplying it. If X is legal, it is supplied by honest businessmen. If X is illegal, then honest men will not traffic in it, because they desire neither to break the law nor go to prison; and the ensuing void will be filled by those willing to step outside the law—outlaws. Either way, X will be supplied. Trebach made the point succinctly: "...no government can repeal the laws of economics..." The state might as well try to repeal the laws of physics.

Neither can the state alter men's moral values. If many individuals desire drugs—or alcohol or prostitution or gambling or one of a dozen other vices—then governmental decree will prove insufficient to annul such urges. Men possess free will; each makes his own choice; and one whose desire for X supersedes his fear of legal retribution will indulge his impulse, regardless of governmental proscription or punishment. *Legal prohibition of vice does not extirpate it; such policy merely drives it underground.*

But the full truth is vastly worse; for the state's War on Drugs is not merely a colossal and colossally expensive failure; it is responsible, both directly and indirectly, for a significant increase in violent crime.

In a direct form, it makes immensely wealthy, and, consequently, immensely powerful, criminal drug cartels of varying nationalities. The bloody gang warfare that inevitably ensues results in an endless string of murders, including of innocent individuals caught in the crossfire. The hideous violence of the illegal drug trade is inescapable, because for outlaws there is no legal method of adjudicating disputes—and, given the character of the thugs involved, it is virtually inconceivable that they would avail themselves of one if there were. Miron pointed out that the data show that "enforcement [of drug prohibition] is consistently associated with higher rates of violence." Indeed, he says, "the estimated impact of enforcement on homicide is not only positive but large; it suggests that eliminating drug prohibition would reduce homicide in the United States by [a staggering] 25 to 75 percent."

Indirectly, the government's War on Drugs contributes to this figure by diverting law enforcement resources away from the struggle against real criminals. Any municipality's criminal justice budget and supply of manpower is finite; to the extent that such resources are devoted to the arrest and incarceration of drug users, to an identical extent they are not deployed in the pursuit and punishment of murderers, rapists, armed robbers, and other violent men.

Or of terrorists.

In practical terms, does it make the slightest sense to spend $40 or $50 billion annually to prevent American adults from using drugs, when fanatical jihadists seek to obliterate U.S. cities? More important: morally, is it right to leave U.S. citizens more vulnerable to terrorist assault, so that drug users may be incarcerated?

The DEA and other federal and state anti-drug agencies employ many tough, smart, honest cops. Such anti-drug agencies must be utterly dismantled; their best cops re-trained to fight jihadists or violent thugs, not drug users; and their full budget devoted to either the anti-jihadist or the anti-violent-criminal campaigns. The result will be a freer and safer America.

Spanish-born philosopher, George Santayana, is frequently quoted for his words: "Those who ignore history are doomed to repeat it." Unfortunately, the U.S. Government has ignored history for many decades; for, since alcohol is a drug, there has been a prior failed war on drugs in America.

The 1920s war on alcohol, Prohibition—or War on Drugs I—was the same abysmal failure as the current War on Drugs II.

Practically, according to some researchers, including Miron, it is possible that Prohibition diminished slightly the consumption of alcohol in America. However, other writers, such as Peter McWilliams in his book, *Ain't Nobody's Business If You Do*, claimed that per capita consumption of alcohol increased dramatically during these years. Nobody knows for certain, because the numerous people drinking covertly at home or in illegal speakeasies were not likely to admit to breaking the law. One point is clear: there was no shortage of available alcohol for people who desired to drink.

But even if Miron's debatable claim is true, two important questions must be asked: (1) Is this a good thing? (2) If it is good, is it worth the immense harm caused in achieving it?

Alcohol in moderation is harmless; perhaps, in the case of red wine, even beneficial, as it might help thin the blood. Certainly, untold millions of adults derive innocent pleasure from moderate alcohol consumption. If alcohol use did, in fact, decline during Prohibition, and did so because responsible adults sought to obey the law, this is a bane, not a blessing; the law, in such cases, accomplished nothing but to rob honest men of an innocuous pleasure.

But even aside from this, the harm caused by Prohibition was nothing short of catastrophic. The main point, of course, is moral: An adult individual has the inalienable right to choose to drink any alcohol he wants, at any time he wishes, in any quantity he prefers. As long as he does not drive, or otherwise put at risk the physical safety and lives of others, it is not the proper business of government to intercede. In such a case, the drinker alone will suffer any negative consequences from excessive indulgence.

Prohibition set a template in America for a massive federal violation of individual rights by means of legal proscription of whatever the U.S. government deems vice.

In practical terms, it made the drinking of alcohol more—not less—dangerous. Most consumers were undeterred by what they rightly considered an unjust law; so demand for liquor remained high. Untrained persons, not professional distillers, now made their own booze, sometimes from wood alcohol, which is dangerous to consume. According to McWilliams, over ten thousand people died from consumption of wood alcohol during Prohibition, and many more went permanently blind.

Further, Prohibition provided the catalyst to organized crime in America. Such otherwise small-time goons as Al Capone, Dutch

Schultz, Lucky Luciano, and others became big-time operators by means of immense profits generated by bootlegging. According to McWilliams, "In one year, Al Capone made $60 million (the equivalent of about $2 billion today) in liquor sales alone..." That kind of income can buy a thug a great deal of influence—and it did. Capone and the others were able to buy off an endless succession of cops, police commissioners, judges, mayors, etc., to look the other way as their illicit enterprises thrived. Political corruption became a way of life in U.S. cities—all because the American people desired to drink, and the American Government refused to permit it.

Crime in America became so organized that by the end of the 1920s, gangsters even held their own convention in Atlantic City. Further, the murder rate rose during these years. According to Miron, "The homicide rate was high in the 1920-1933 period, when constitutional prohibition of alcohol was in effect [significantly higher than in the years prior to 1920]...After repeal of alcohol prohibition, the homicide rate dropped quickly..." With enormous bootlegging profits at stake, and rival gangs of violent hoods vying for control of the illicit industry, a rising homicide rate is lamentably predictable; equally predictable is its decline when prohibition is repealed, the thugs are thereby disenfranchised, and the alcohol trade is once again controlled by honest businessmen.

There is a *Law of Unintended Consequences* that governments consistently overlook. When individual rights are violated, many individuals, in support of their values, take actions that bring results the government neither foresaw nor desired. So, for example, when the U.S. Government banned alcohol, millions of drinkers covertly continued their indulgence, thousands of illegal "speakeasies" were established in the nation's cities, mobsters made immense fortunes supplying the demand, and the criminal justice system was infected by pervasive corruption. The current War on Drugs constitutes a similar example.

Making men's values illegal does not alter their values. It merely alters the methods by which they attain those values.

What will result if the prohibition of drugs is repealed—and the right of adults to indulge them is protected?

The profoundly positive benefits that will ensue are multiple.

First and most important: full legalization of all drugs protects the inalienable right of each consenting adult to choose for himself which such substances, if any, he will ingest. The coercive power of the state

163

to violate individual rights, to dictate to innocent men the scope of their legitimate action is, on this issue, thereby prohibited. A proper morality, banning the initiation of force in all forms, is upheld. The progress toward a civilized society, one respecting and legally protecting the right of all honest men to conduct their lives via their own judgment, is promoted. The sacred cause of freedom is advanced.

Because the moral is the practical, numerous utilitarian purposes are achieved.

A first and manifest virtue is that legalization removes drug trafficking from the clutches of the most vile, violent gangsters on earth. It keeps enormous wealth and consequent power out of the hands of such maleficent creatures. It greatly reduces the hideous mayhem and obscene murder rates that inevitably result from prohibition enforcement.

If all drug prohibition laws are repealed, then drugs can be sold in nonpharmaceutical drug stores, just as liquor is sold in liquor stores. One immense benefit is that honest businessmen would then supply drugs, the way they do alcohol; since no covert smuggling is required, criminal gangs would be disenfranchised. Their source of wealth and power is thereby depleted; if they continue as vile mobsters, they can be hunted down, arrested, and/or killed; and in the absence of enormous revenues generated by illicit drug smuggling, their services would not be replicated.

A second boon is that law enforcement assets can then be deployed exceptionlessly in the struggle against terrorists and violent criminals, not squandered in a futile attempt to prevent American adults from ingesting drugs.

Most important, by expunging the immoral, impractical war on drugs, repeal facilitates a moral and practical war on them. The question among many honest men will then be: How can we prevent otherwise innocent individuals from killing themselves on toxic drugs?

The key to an answer lies in recognizing that this issue is a matter of personal values. How to convince a drug user to alter his values?

One thing a clean living man can do to help his brothers and sisters is to achieve a life of shining value fulfillment. He can realize himself in education, career, romance, family, friends, physical fitness, travel, etc. He can fill his existence with reality-adhering, life-promoting values, thereby experiencing profound happiness. *He can set an example, accessible to all with eyes to see, of what a healthy, happy, drug-free life looks like.*

To consistently talk the talk, one must antecedently walk the walk. Based on such a life, the clean liver is free to use rational persuasion to reach any individual within his purview with a single unrelenting message: *Values are the meaning of life.* Rational values produce flourishing life; toxic drugs produce premature death. The clean liver thereby appeals to the best within men: their reasoning mind. He respects their right of choice. Rather than coerce them, he reasons with them. In deeds, he is a paragon of value achievement; in words, a lofty spokesman for it.

An effectual war on drugs is necessarily not a legal struggle—but an intellectual, educational, moral one. We must teach our children, our students, our friends, our neighbors the code of rational egoism; that a man's life belongs to him, that attainment of personal happiness is sacred, that happiness is gained by unswerving pursuit of life-enhancing values, and that an individual must never sacrifice, betray, or surrender those values. Such a code urges value achievement and joy; it is inspiring; it galvanizes men and uplifts them. Why should an individual risk death for a few moments of pleasure from toxic drugs when a rich life of education, career, love, children, friends, etc., is his to be gained?

Conversely, the code of self-sacrifice dominant in our culture is the remorseless enemy of a rational war on drugs, and a prime cause of widespread drug abuse.

The reason is that if a man truly *sacrifices* for others, as contrasted with benignly helping another person, then he surrenders something of value to him. It is not a sacrifice if an individual gives to others a few moments of his time, a few dollars of his wealth, a few units of his energy. But if he surrenders his education, his career, his love, etc.—something of immense value—this is a sacrifice.

A code of self-sacrifice militates against values—against those things and/or persons that bring meaning, fulfillment, and joy into an individual's life.

Such a code is impossible to practice, because, consistently deployed, it would lead to death. The overwhelming majority of honest men, especially in America, do not even try to practice it. But when a death-dealing theory is the only moral code proclaimed in a society—and universally expressed by family, government, school, and church—that is, by what might be dubbed the "Moral Establishment"—then millions of individuals are indoctrinated with the creed that a moral life consists exclusively of drab duty, selfless service, and relinquishing of personal values. They are taught that

165

the pursuit of personal values that makes them happy is "selfish," i.e., immoral or at best amoral. Is it any wonder that, in consequence, millions of individuals are clinically depressed, afflicted with alcohol or drug problems, and/or deeply troubled in numerous other forms?

Teach men a code of death and, in countless forms, they will "achieve" premature death, not flourishing life. Conversely, teach men a code of life, and they will shun death-dealing substances and proceed to joyously prosper.

Drug abuse is a matter of personal values. Personal values cannot be altered by legislation, but only by means of choosing more rational values. The elimination of drug abuse can be achieved only by the drug abuser voluntarily changing his lifestyle—to adopt life-sustaining values he learns from rational men, via countless forums, in a free society of open discussion. Whether from the lives and/or words of healthy men, or through participation in rehabilitation programs, or reading *The Fountainhead* and/or *Atlas Shrugged*—or any combination of these—or in another form—the self-destructive man must learn life-promoting values from healthy individuals who practice them.

If honest men genuinely desire to terminate drug abuse, they must first lead a drug-free life—and then reach out to their self-destructive brethren, via rational persuasion, proclaiming such a life's virtues. This is the sole moral and practical way to fight a war on drugs.

Will some still kill themselves on toxic substances? It is highly (and tragically) likely that some will continue to make death-inducing choices regardless the pervasiveness of a life-giving creed within their compass. But that life-giving creed will save many who would otherwise kill themselves in a society that remorselessly preaches a code of self-sacrifice—and then conducts a coercive war against those pathetic souls who defy that code by courting bodily pleasures that are, in fact, self-destructive.

The code of rational egoism provides the necessary foundation of a war on drugs that is simultaneously moral and effectual. *It exhilarates men; it does not depress them.* It is long past time for the Moral Establishment to teach it to every man, woman, and child in the country.

Immigration

Open the borders!

As a general rule, immigrants have greatly enriched this country—and continue to. America's borders must be overwhelmingly, although not universally, open.

Above all, this is a moral issue. It is the inalienable right of any honest individual to reside in any country he chooses. He is an upstanding person; he does good, not ill; consequently, there is every moral reason supporting his right to choice of nation, and no moral reason opposing it.

Further, what does it mean to be a free country? It means to respect and protect the inalienable right to life, liberty, property, and the pursuit of happiness possessed by every man—whether native born or foreigner, whether a U.S. citizen or a citizen of another land. The government of a free country must, as a strictly logical point, *in order to be the government of a free country*, recognize and protect the right of all honest men to choose their country of residence; it must uphold their right of immigration and emigration; and it must protect the right of honest immigrants to become citizens of the free nation. Just as men are free to emigrate from a free nation, so they must be free to immigrate to it.

Additionally, the government of a free country must defend its citizens and residents from any and all who would initiate force, whether domestic or foreign. Morally, the government of a free nation must defend its people against the country's sworn enemies.

Today, the overwhelming threat to American lives—indeed, to the nation's very existence—is Islamic Totalitarianism, and the terrorism it spawns. It would be irresponsibly immoral on the part of the U.S. Government to subject Americans to graver danger by failing to rigorously screen immigration from the Arab-Islamic lands that spawn America's enemies. Until the day that America obliterates Islamic Totalitarianism, both militarily and intellectually—and thereby de-fangs the Islamic faith, as described in Chapter Two—it must be made exceedingly difficult, although not impossible, for individuals from Islamic lands to emigrate to America. The tens of billions of dollars annually spent in the current War on Drugs, and the law enforcement resources thereby deployed, should properly be used performing background checks to ensure that prospective immigrants from Islamic countries are not supporters of jihad in any form—and to more stringently examine the backgrounds of immigrants from non-Islamic lands to ensure absence of any criminal past.

A generally open borders policy is morally right—but open borders do not necessitate unexamined immigrants.

Indeed, protecting the rights and lives of Americans requires that immigrants be examined more scrupulously than ever.

167

For those who believe that the expense of ensuring honest immigrants—those who are neither jihadists nor criminals—is too great, it must be pointed out that, as an important practical point, the intellectual/material wealth created by immigrants vastly exceeds such expenditure. This is true both historically and currently.

Historically, remember, Andrew Carnegie was a Scottish immigrant; John Roebling, a German one; Nikola Tesla, a Serb who emigrated from Croatia; Albert Einstein was a German immigrant who became a U.S. citizen in 1940; the great economist, Ludwig von Mises, was an Austrian immigrant; and Ayn Rand, whose given name was Alyssa Rosenbaum, a Russian one. The list could be indefinitely extended.

Jason Riley, in his book, *Let Them In: The Case For Open Borders*, pointed out that, more recently, "in 2003, the foreign-born share of Ph.D.s working in science and engineering nationwide was 30 percent." T.J. Rodgers, founder and CEO of Cypress Semiconductor, wrote in *The Wall Street Journal* that a "disproportionate number of our research-and-development engineers—37 percent—are immigrants, typical for Silicon Valley." Rodgers went on to note that had Cypress been prevented from hiring those 172 foreign-born engineers, it would have been unable to create roughly 860 other jobs, more than two-thirds of which are in the United States.

Sergey Brin, co-founder of Google, emigrated to the United States from the Soviet Union. Jerry Yang, co-founder of Yahoo, emigrated to America from Taiwan. Vinod Khosla, one of the founders of Sun Microsystems is an Indian immigrant; Andreas Bechtolsheim, another of Sun's founders, a German one. Riley wrote that in 2004, "children of immigrants were 65 percent of the Math Olympiad's top scorers and 46 percent of the U.S. Physics team." Further, also in 2004, the Intel Science Talent Search saw seven of its top ten award winners and 60 percent of its finalists come from immigrants or their children. In the terms of economics, such brilliant minds represent immense human capital. This list, too, could be indefinitely expanded.

Immigrants, whether high-or-low-skilled, whether in the country legally or illegally, tend to have a strong work ethic. For example, Linda Chavez, publishing in 1993, pointed out that Haitians, Jamaicans, Salvadorans, Guatemalans, Peruvians, and Filipinos had "labor force participation rates at least ten points higher than those of the native-born."

In 2005, immigrants composed but 12 percent of the U.S. population—but 15 percent of the work force. (Riley wrote that roughly one-third of these immigrant workers were in the country illegally.) There is a compelling reason for this: even today, when the country enacts welfare programs not in existence a century ago, the overwhelming majority of those who pack up and ship out of the society in which they were born and raised, attained linguistic fluency—and gained friends, family, and a general comfort level—are *rationally ambitious individuals.* The United States is the favored destination of such rationally ambitious persons because they recognize that *America is the greatest country on earth*—and is so, not because it has welfare programs but because its mixed economy contains more elements of capitalism and fewer of statism than any other nation. America is still freer than any other country; consequently, it is wealthier than any other; therefore, the opportunities there are greatest. In short, most immigrants come to gain better lives for themselves and their families—and this is achieved not by refusing to work but by a willingness to work harder than most others.

Nathan Glazer made this exact point in the context of identifying the main difficulty of attempting to successfully restrict immigration: "Whatever our policies are, however...our biggest problem will be to carry them out in a world in which so many see entry into the United States as a way of improving themselves."

Low-skilled immigrants, many of whom are Latinos, some of whom do not speak English, in case after case, take low-paying jobs that native-born Americans are unwilling to fill. For example, in 2005, roughly 45 percent of workers without a high-school education were immigrants, many of them Latino. The recipe for success among many immigrants has long been and remains: take scut work that most native-born Americans refuse to perform, toil for longer hours, and work for lower pay than native-born citizens will; and thereby claw out a better life than was possible in the repressed and/or destitute land left behind.

For example, Thomas Sowell pointed out in *Ethnic America* that, at the turn of the twentieth century, Italian immigrants worked generally as streetsweepers, sewer diggers, garbage collectors, rag pickers, etc., rather than at jobs that required higher degrees of skill or education. "Sheer willingness to work remained a potent force in their economic rise..." Further, although American Jews have generally been affluent for several generations, Jewish immigrants of a century ago were desperately poor. Sowell stated: "The [East European Jews] were not only poorer—most arrived destitute, *with less money than any other immigrant group...*" The Jews rose initially, overwhelmingly, not as educated professionals but as "sweat shop" workers in the garment industry. "In a sense, Jews are the classic American [immigrant] success story—from rags to riches against all opposition" and done "in a relatively short period of history." (Emphasis added.)

Speaking of current low-skilled immigrant workers, Riley noted; "By heading north, a typical Mexican immigrant can nearly quadruple his hourly wage, and that's even adjusting for cost-of-living differences...The average Mexican worker sends home 41 percent of his pay..." supporting his destitute family. Riley's conclusion supports that of Linda Chavez's nearly 20 years ago: "We know from labor force participation rates that low-skill immigrants are society's hardest workers."

Should America become a country denying a home to humanity's hardest workers? Or should it open its magnanimous arms and clasp such workers to its bosom? Which policy is in America's long-term self-interest?

Such immigrant willingness—then and now—to work at jobs generally scorned by the native born is a universal win. The immigrants get to live and work in America, with greater freedom and higher living standards than in the nations they abandoned—and their children and grandchildren tend to outstrip them both educationally and economically. American employers get a supply of cheap labor, willing to perform any task, no matter how menial. American consumers enjoy the lower prices that result from a cheap labor supply. Low-skilled native-born workers competing for jobs with immigrants—who enjoy the immense advantage of speaking fluent English and of knowing the culture thoroughly—are incentivized to upgrade their skills.

Additionally, Riley cited an academic study showing that "lower-skilled laborers are job multipliers..." For example, "each farm worker creates three jobs in the surrounding economy—in equipment and sales and processing and packaging." The same is true in other industries.

In addition to the economic gain, there is an important security benefit to an open immigration policy. Since it is a great boon to an immigrant to be in the country legally rather than illegally, the overwhelming majority of them, given the choice, will walk in through the front door, thereby initiating the process of becoming a U.S. citizen. The flood of migrant workers seeking to illegally sneak into the United States across the Mexican border will be reduced to a trickle. *The money and manpower currently used to keep Mexican workers out of the country can then be used to keep Middle Eastern Islamic terrorists out of the country.* Related, an open immigration policy enables immigrants to get such legal documents as a driver's license, social security number and card, etc., thereby making it vastly easier for law-enforcement agencies to track their whereabouts and activities.

One objection to open immigration that must be answered is the claim that immigrants will come in with their hands out, looking to exist on the dole, and leech the wealth of native-born U.S. citizens. One answer to this objection has already been provided: the overwhelming preponderance of immigrants have a strong work ethic, are producers, not parasites, and add immensely to the nation's intellectual/material wealth.

But there is a more important response. *The welfare state must be phased out, regardless of the country's immigration policy.* The coercive redistribution of wealth is a moral obscenity. For one, it robs productive men of their hard-earned wealth, forcing them to support the lives of others. For another, it turns the recipients of such stolen loot into wards of the state, placing perverse financial incentives in support of men's most irrational and indolent premises. For example, the backbone of the welfare state was Aid to Families with Dependent Children (AFDC). Once having accepted AFDC, with its self-destructive incentives, *the average family's stay on it was thirteen years.* Tragically, if the state makes handouts financially equivalent (or even superior) to minimum wage employment, then many people will permit themselves to be seduced onto the dole, thereby diminishing the personal responsibility they need in order to lead successful, fulfilling lives.

A welfare state is a lose–lose policy. Even if the government must provide grace periods in which, after an allotted time, welfare benefits are reduced and, gradually, within a five or even ten-year period, phased out—thus giving wards of the state ample time to adjust to a self-supporting life—the morally proper goal must be its utter obliteration. In reality, poverty is not like an incurable disease. It is a problem cured by full-time employment. Voluntary support from friends, family members, and private charity organizations will suffice for those few unable to work. As cited in the earlier chapter on education, America is an immensely charitable nation. Eliminate the welfare state, and the taxes levied to support it, and such voluntary giving to worthy causes will only increase.

With fewer producers robbed to support the indolent—with more jobs thereby created—and many more persons now working productively, the practical gains will be manifest. Both the former welfare providers and former recipients will live wealthier, more fulfilling lives—and all sectors of the U.S. economy will benefit.

In short, the U.S. welfare state is, overwhelmingly, a problem of native-born Americans—including of Washington's welfare pimps and their intellectual supporters—and, for reasons both moral and practical, must be abolished. It is not a problem to be conflated with the question of open immigration.

Gay Marriage

If the moral principle of inalienable individual rights is to be taken seriously, and universally applied, then homosexuals have as much right to love and marriage as do heterosexuals.

In his book, *Gay Marriage*, Jonathan Rauch made the point succinctly: "'All men are created equal,' says the Declaration of Independence...' 'They are endowed by their Creator with certain unalienable rights...among these are life, liberty, and the pursuit of happiness.' For homosexuals no less than heterosexuals, home and family...are at the heart of the pursuit of happiness...Marriage is an irreplaceable ingredient in the quest for home and family...and so, if the Declaration's words mean anything, they suggest that to deprive millions of Americans of any hope of an emotionally satisfying relationship—marriage—is unjust..."

Governments must prohibit all acts that initiate force or fraud against another. Conversely, they must protect the right of consenting adults to perform whatever acts they will, including a marriage between partners of the same gender.

No one's rights are violated by a same-sex marriage between consenting adults. In such a case, everyone's rights are upheld. But the rights of adult homosexuals are violated by the government's ban on same-sex marriage.

As always, the practical gains of respecting individual rights will be significant. For homosexuals, growing up in a society that respects gay marriage, and a legal system that recognizes and protects it, helps to legitimize the right, as consenting adults, to their sexual preferences. Many homosexuals, growing up and living in a basically heterosexual world, understandably agonize over coming to terms with their own homosexuality. Widespread acceptance of the institution of gay marriage, including its legal recognition, over a period of decades, will help to ameliorate such unnecessary suffering.

Further, as Rauch pointed out, love, and lovemaking, and marriage properly go together. It is not that unmarried consenting adults cannot form romantic relationships, gain a healthy intimacy in all respects, and hold the moral high ground in so doing—it is that marriage states to each partner, and to the world, the finality of each person's choice. "We are family in the fullest, deepest sense," states the commitment to marry, "and we will be together until one of us is carried out in a box." Such depth of commitment, when carried through lovingly over the course of a lifetime, provides human beings the greatest trust, intimacy, and togetherness they will ever find. You face life and all its adversities as a team, as a unit, and you are never alone in times joyous or difficult. In terms of human relationships, there is no greater height to be achieved. Should an entire segment of the human population be denied it simply because the majority does not share (or perhaps disapproves of) their sexual orientation?

Related, homosexual culture is notorious for sexual promiscuity (especially among males). But if the sexual activities of a group of people is socially scorned and driven underground—if their loving, affectionate, open relationships are derided and unaccepted—and if the sacred institution of marriage is legally denied them—is any other result to be expected? Social recognition of homosexual love, and the legalization of same-sex marriage do not form a universal panacea for the ills of homosexual culture, but they represent enormous forward motion. For the social message then delivered to young gays growing up is that openly loving relationships and lifetime marriages are, for you, properly, as attainable, and good, and rewarding, and recognized as they are for heterosexuals. What set of policies could better promote committed relationships and sexual fidelity than these?

Additionally, there are many gay couples who raise children, whether from previous marriages, adoption, or insemination. The Census Bureau estimated in 2000 that roughly 28 percent of gay households had children—just over one-third of lesbian couples and slightly more than one-fifth of male couples. Such households reared a minimum of 166,000 children, and possibly more than 300,000. A good deal of research establishes that children do best when their parents are in a stable relationship—and marriage is a stabilizing influence on relationships. The legalization of gay marriage would result in the matrimony of some of these couples, with generally positive consequences for the children.

173

Marriage also creates kin, a fact especially important for couples less likely to have children than heterosexuals. Such intimacy ensures a larger number of caregivers for homosexuals as they transition into old age. As Rauch poignantly observed: "...no institution or government program can begin to match the love of a devoted partner."

Further, although a culture of marital commitment might not have been sufficient to obviate the AIDS crisis, it surely would have helped slow the disease's lethal spread, thereby saving many innocent lives.

Rauch makes another important point. For anyone who believes that committed, loving marriage is the most fulfilling form of emotional life for the vast majority of human beings, and want to encourage people to marry—not merely to co-habitate—then it is dangerous to set up a whole segment of the population, composing millions of persons, as "walking billboards for the irrelevance of marriage."

Some conservative intellectuals loudly yowl that marriage, by definition, is a specific relationship between a man and a woman. But their arguments are based in tradition and in faith. Marriage, in fact, is a lifetime relationship between adults that properly involves love, commitment, intimacy, and care giving—and it is a legally recognized lifetime relationship. Such a relationship might bear children or it might not. Such a relationship might exist between a man and a woman—or a woman and a woman—or a man and a man. There is no rational basis on which to exclude men or women from marrying a partner of the same gender. As always regarding actions between consenting adults, that involve no initiation of force or fraud, these are matters that must be left to the discretion of the individuals involved; these are not issues regarding which society as a whole—or, and especially, the government—has any proper say.

If the right of adult homosexuals to marry is legally upheld, they could benefit enormously—and the rights of no individual are violated. This, in short, is the case for the legalization of gay marriage.

Epilogue

Re-Stating the Theme

The book's theme can be re-stated succinctly: in all cases, consistent protection of individual rights and establishment of a free market constitute the solution to America's current dilemmas. There are no exceptions.

Related: because the moral is the practical—and the immoral is the impractical—the unbreached protection of individual rights leads to extensive real-life benefits. Similarly, the abrogation of individual rights—to the extent such rights are violated—leads to predictable, at times cataclysmic harm. The nation's choice is, therefore, stark: individual rights and immense intellectual/material prosperity—or abrogation of individual rights and severely diminished intellectual/material prosperity; greater freedom and flourishing life—or less freedom and the diminishment of flourishing life. The choice, in other words, is: the moral and the practical—or the immoral and the impractical.

Explained in such terms, the right choice, for any rational individual, is not difficult to discern.

Index